THE GASLIGHT EFFECT

A Powerful Guide on How to Survive Secret Manipulation and Narcissistic Abuse.
Learn How to Disarm Manipulative People, Free Yourself, and Conquer Secret Control of Others

TRAVIS EMOTION

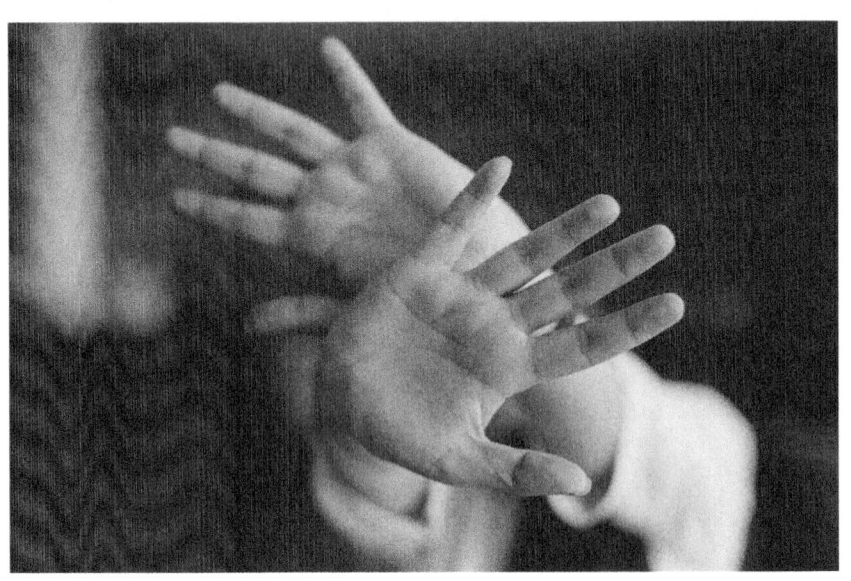

Copyright © 2021 - All rights reserved
Author: *Travis Emotion*
ISBN: 9798497714463

This document is geared towards providing exact and reliable information with regard to the topic and issue covered. The publication is sold with the idea that the publisher is not required to render accounting, officially permitted or otherwise qualified services. If advice is necessary, legal or professional, a practiced individual in the profession should be ordered.
- From a Declaration of Principles which was accepted and approved equally by a Committee of the American Bar Association and a Committee of Publishers and Associations.

In no way is it legal to reproduce, duplicate, or transmit any part of this document in either electronic means or in printed format. All rights reserved.

The information provided herein is stated to be truthful and consistent, in that any liability, in terms of inattention or otherwise, by any usage or abuse of any policies, processes, or directions contained within is the solitary and utter responsibility of the recipient reader. Under no circumstances will any legal responsibility or blame be held against the publisher for any reparation, damages, or monetary loss due to the information herein, either directly or indirectly.

Respective authors own all copyrights not held by the publisher.

The information herein is offered for informational purposes solely and is universal as so. The presentation of the information is without a contract or any type of guarantee assurance.

The trademarks that are used are without any consent, and the publication of the trademark is without permission or backing by the trademark owner. All trademarks and brands within this book are for clarifying purposes only and are owned by the owners themselves, not affiliated with this document.

ABOUT THE AUTHOR

Travis Emotion was born in San Francisco in 1973 and is a well-known American psychologist who specializes in subconscious study.

He comes from a very humble family. The reason that pushed him to become a well-known psychologist lies in his personal history.

Travis's mother was diagnosed with schizophrenia when he was only 14 years old.

At that time, he realized how fragile the mind of human beings could be. He begins to study psychology in a desperate attempt to help his mother, but you know, a 14-year-old boy can do nothing alone against such a severe illness.

So, as soon as he finishes high school, he moves to Los Angeles to attend the College of Psychology, where he graduates with honors.

Now he lives with his wife and children in the San Francisco Bay Area. He carries out his study of psychology. For several years he has been conducting experiments to understand the true potential of the unconscious mind.

His mother's schizophrenia has never passed, but on the other hand, she has had significant improvements, and now she lives almost everyday life.

Travis's mission is to unlock the potential hidden in the mind of as many people as possible through refined techniques of unconscious mind reprogramming. He provides strategic resources to guide you on an extraordinary journey towards total self-control of cognitive behavior and emotions. As a result, you will learn to develop the true potential that you had hidden in your mind.

So, no one will ever be able to influence your choices and decisions again. The solution is relatively simple.

Becoming aware of habits from our minds is the key to developing our mental abilities and controlling our subconscious.

Controlling and modifying the subconscious opens the door to a gradual process of transformation of habits that allow you to have greater control of life, communication with others, and personal relationships.

Travis Emotion will help you to find the keys to your change towards a better life.

Thank you so much for downloading my book. I know you have not read my book yet, but reviews are important to me and the success of my book. If you like what you see, could you please take a minute to leave a review on Amazon with your feedback once to get to the end.

Table of Contents

Introduction 10

Chapter 1. What is Gaslighting? 14
- *Gaslighting Defies Boundaries* 15
- *Setting Up an Angry Beast* 17
- *Hijacking the Issue* 18

Chapter 2. How Did It Come to Be the Favorite Tool of Manipulation for a Narcissist? 20
- *Constant Need for Attention and Validation* 22
- *Demand for Control All the Time* 22
- *Entitlement* 23
- *Refusing Responsibility* 23
- *Absence of Empathy* 23
- *Invulnerability* 24
- *Inability to Work as Part of a Team* 24

Chapter 3. Are Gaslighting and Narcissism the Same? 28
- *What Is Narcissism?* 28
- *Characteristics of a Narcissist* 30
- *Are Gaslighting and Narcissism the Same?* 33

Chapter 4. Basics and Types of Narcissistic Abuse 35
- *Narcissistic Emotional Dependent* 36
- *Narcissistic Tyrant* 37
- *Elitist Narcissistic* 37
- *Fantasy Narcissistic* 38
- *Somatic Narcissistic* 38
- *Narcissistic Antagonist* 39
- *Narcissist Trickster* 39
- *Narcissistic Martyr* 40

Messianic Narcissistic *40*
Vengeful Narcissism *41*
Tactics Narcissists Will Use to Manipulate You *41*
Triangulation *42*
Devaluation *43*
Aggression *43*
Decrease *44*
Playing the Victim *44*
Inappropriate Behavior *44*
Conversation Monopoly *44*
Projection *45*
Brainwashing *45*
Gaslighting *45*
Verbal Aggression *45*

Chapter 5. Acknowledging Abuse and Recovery Recommended Activities 46

Your Inner Talk *47*
Thought-Awareness Exercise *48*
Self-Interview Exercise *49*
Mirror Work *50*
Shift Your Self-Perception *52*
Do Something Off-Limits *53*
Help Others *53*
Emulate Habits from Role Models and Mentors *54*
One More Thing… Be on the Lookout for the "Hoovering" Tactics *54*

Chapter 6. The Narcissist/Gaslighter Explored 56

What Is A Narcissist? *56*
Narcissism and Gaslighting *58*
The Art of Making Others Crazy *60*
Making People do What the Narcissist Wants *62*

Chapter 7. Signs of Emotional Abuse 65

When You are Habitually Lied To *66*
When You Start Withholding Information from Friends and Family *68*
They Compare You to Others *68*
You Constantly second-guess Yourself *69*

You Have a Sense of Becoming a Totally Different Person 70
When Friends Try Saving You from Yourself 70
You Feel as Though You Can't Do Anything Right 70
They Isolate You 70
It Is a One-sided Loyalty 71

Chapter 8. How to Avoid Mental Manipulation and the Narcissist's Favorite Tool for Manipulation 72

Stop Falling into Their Traps 73
Start Noting Down Everything They Say While Conversing with You .. 73
Try Steering Clear Whenever It is Possible 74
Try Keeping a Backup 75
Start Calling Them Out on Their Behavior 75
Don't Get Emotionally Attached to Them 76
Try Meditating Often 77
Try Inspiring Them 77
Try Not to Get Too Empathetic 78
Start Telling Them That They Are Right 78
Try Letting Go of the Harmful Relationships 79
Develop a Strong Mentality 80
Practice Positive Self-Talk 80

Chapter 9. Why We Fall, Victim? 82

Things about You That Make You a Target 83
How the Narcissist Tests You 86
Sometimes There's No Reason 88

Chapter 10. The Road To Recovery 90

Cutting Ties and Moving On 91
Building Boundaries 96

Chapter 11. 5 Powerful Self-Care Tips for Abuse and Trauma Survivors 100

Respect Yourself 101
Acceptance 101
Distinguish Your Mistakes 102
Pay Attention with Your Critical Voice 102

Please, Do Not Seek the Approval of Others *103*

Chapter 12. Healing from Emotional Trauma and Rebuilding Your Life 108

Seek Professional Help *109*
Permit Yourself to Feel *109*
Never Go for Revenge *110*
Seek Self-Affirmation *111*
Shift Your Perspective *112*
Develop New Relations *112*
Take Your Time *113*
Use Meditation to Enhance Empathy *113*

Conclusion 116

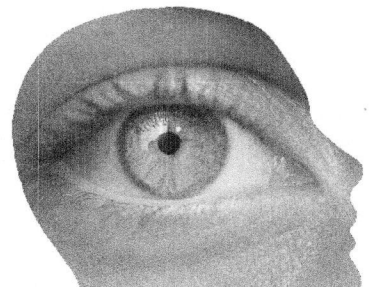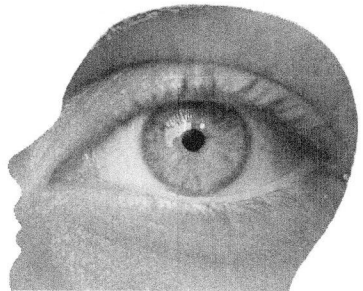

Introduction

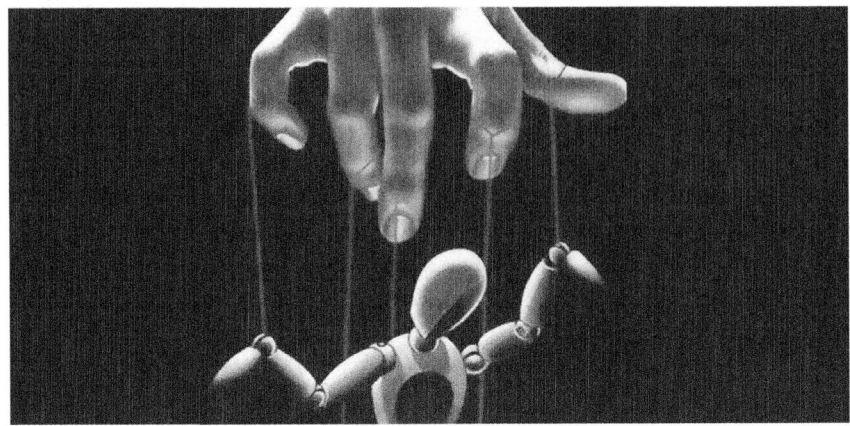

Congratulations on purchasing *The Gaslighting Effect,* and thank you for doing so. There are plenty of books on this subject on the market so, thanks again for choosing this one! Every effort was made to ensure it was as full of helpful information as possible; please enjoy!

Have you ever confronted a significant other knowing that what he did was blatantly wrong, yet you leave the conversation feeling overly emotional or crazy or guilty? If so, chances are you've experienced gaslighting.

Gaslighting is a quieter form of emotional abuse that abusers use to make victims question their own sanity. When a narcissist wants to control you, he'll do something that's super wrong. There won't be a question in your mind that what he did was foul. But somehow, he'll make you believe that you somehow did him wrong.

What's the Purpose of Gaslighting?

Narcissists are quite miserable people. Every day, they wake up with one goal in mind: To get as much fuel as they possibly can.

What is "fuel," you ask? Fuel is the jolt of energy that a narcissist gets from other people's reactions. Every time he does something to make you mad, it gives him fuel. When you cry from the pain that he's caused, he gets fuel. When you praise him, it gives him fuel? In other words, the narcissist does things purposely to incite extreme emotional reactions so that he can get energy from it. Think of him as a bit of a toddler who absolutely has to have the attention focused on him at all costs. He doesn't care if he gets that attention from you being mad as hell or happy as hell… just as long as he gets it.

Your pain, anger, and admiration are what the narcissist needs to thrive. And if he can't get those things from you, he has no problem getting it elsewhere until you come around.

Now that you know how narcissists are intrinsically motivated, you'll understand why gaslighting is one of the most prevalent mind games that a narcissist play.

The narcissist knows if he can make you think that you are the one who's in the wrong, the guilt or doubt you feel will be enough to make your stay in the relationship.

When the narc gaslights you, he's doing it for two reasons:

- He is trying to escape blame, so he figures that shifting it to you is his best option.
- He wants to diminish your self-esteem to a point where you subconsciously put him on a pedestal (your need for the narc's approval will make him feel more powerful)

How do I know If It's Happening to Me?

If you're absolutely sure that you're dating a narcissist, then he's definitely gaslighting you. There's no way that a narcissist can carry on a relationship without gaslighting. If they did, you'd literally be able to see everything that they did wrong, and you'd leave. But if the narcissist makes you believe that you're the wrong or crazy one, you're less compelled to leave the relationship.

However, convinced you may be that you're dating a narcissist, you can be sure that you're still going to have some doubt about whether or not some of the things he's blamed you for are really your fault. That's the purpose of this book. I want to show you what he's doing instead of merely trying to tell you.

How Does A Narcissist Carry Out The Gaslighting Technique?

He does it in three main ways:
- By reversing the roles so that you're the wrong one
- By making himself seem misunderstood or misheard so that you doubt your own opinion
- By making you think that you're crazy so that you doubt your own feelings

As the pages go on, I'll show you how the narcissist skillfully uses these techniques and, most importantly, how you can avoid becoming a victim.

Chapter 1.
WHAT IS GASLIGHTING?

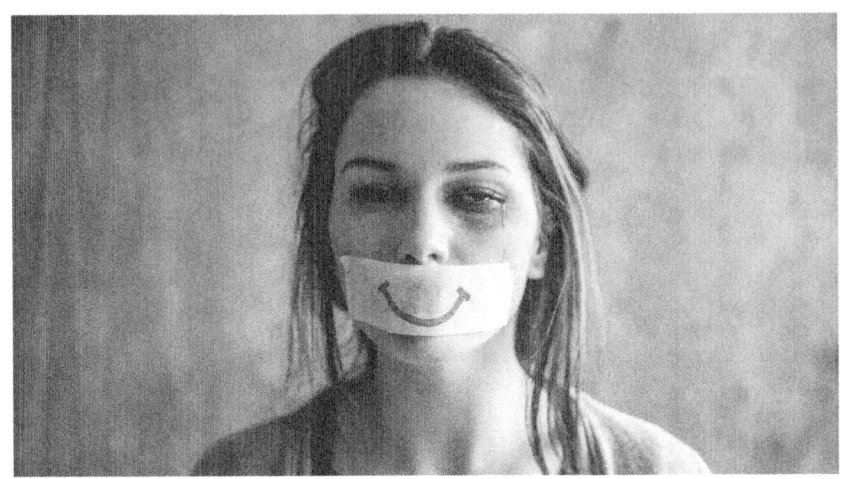

Gaslighting is the undertaking of another person to wind your existence. Narcissists can't and don't accept obligation for their direct. Maybe, they hope to shame and blame others for sidestepping the terrible sentiments. This is sometimes alluded to as projection.

The issue is, gaslighting is elusive. It plays on our most incredibly terrible sensations of fear, our most anxious insights, and our most significant wishes to be fathomed, recognized, and adored. Right, when someone we trust, respect, or love converses with unimaginable conviction—mainly if there's a hint of authenticity in his words, or if he's hit on one of our "red catches"—it will, in general, be troublesome not to confide in him. Besides, when we celebrate the trickster—when we need to believe him to be the affection for our life, an excellent chief, or a splendid parent—at that point, we make it harder to cling to our feeling of the real world. Our swindler ought to be right; we need to win his support; accordingly, the gaslighting goes on. Neither of you may think about what's really happening. The gaslighter may acknowledge each word he tells you or truly feel that he's simply saving you from yourself. Remember: His own requirements are driving him.

Your trickster may give off an impression of being a strong, powerful man or having every one of the reserves of being a problematic, angry outburst throwing young fellow; regardless, he feels delicate and weak. To feel notable and safe, he needs to exhibit that he is right, and he needs to get you to agree with him. At that point, you have respected your backstabber and are restless for his support, even though you may not purposefully get this.

However, suppose there's even a smidgen of you that accepts. In that case, you're terrible enough without any other person—if even a little piece of you trusts you need your gaslighter's affection or support to be satisfied—by then, you are frail to gaslight. Additionally, a swindler will abuse that weakness to make you question yourself, over and over.

Gaslighting Defies Boundaries

At the point when someone is gaslighting you, they are attempting to persuade you that your limits and insights are ludicrous and invalid.

If something they say troubles you since it is oppressive or false, they will disclose to you that you are blowing up or that what you are saying is inept. They will reveal to you that it doesn't trouble any other individual aside from you and that you're simply being excessively delicate. Indeed, even profound individuals are not safe from this since you may be informed that their conduct wouldn't trouble you on the off chance that you were more illuminated. In this way, generally, gaslighting and control methods make you question your limits or make you drop your limits out and out by persuading you that your boundaries are dumb and invalid.

In all actuality, your limits aren't anyone's business; however, yours. No one will figure out what limits you will have. In the case of something that pesters you, at that point, no one will disclose to you how you feel. At the point when you authorize a limit, you are battling for the actual limit, be that as it may, all the more critically, for your entitlement to define limits in any case. Try not to allow someone else to persuade you that your limit isn't large enough for you to stand firm—finished. It is. Such a perspective is truly impolite.

It's extremely impolite and disrespectful to remain on another person's limit. There is a contrast between controlling another person by disclosing to them how to carry on and defining a boundary by which you are advising the individual not to act a specific method to you. Supporting a limit implies that you must leave somebody or something when they plan something incorrectly for you. Presently, understand that it's not tied in with preventing somebody from carrying on with their everyday routine how they need to experience their life, nor is it removing their independence from them. It's just about deciding to draw in with or not draw in with individuals who act with a particular goal in mind or who don't regard your limits.

Setting Up an Angry Beast

The second type of control is to turn into a furious monster. This is the place where someone attempts to get angrier than you when you blow up with them, to crush your test or disobedience. You may even be simply somewhat irritated about something and need to converse with your accomplice about it; however, they detonate at you, so you wind up withdrawing. You will be so stunned because you were looking at something which was generally small, and they just transformed it into something gigantic. You will need to withdraw and not arrange that kind of show. Regularly, you will be attempting to guard your limits, and that is the thing that causes the blast.

This furious monster will come at you with a passionate reaction that is way messed up with the circumstance or position you're attempting to shield. You will withdraw, and, regularly, you will make an effort not to defend yourself again because you are in no way, shape, or form willing to go facing that furious monster. The backstabber depends on that.

Yet, when you are guarding a legitimate limit or defining a limit, it doesn't actually matter what the limit is about, nor does it truly matter if that individual considers it to be substantial.

When you have plainly imparted a limit, and the other individual says that he won't acknowledge it, you should finish the outcomes, or you will be scared into quiet and accommodation. That is the thing that the irate monster needs.

Hijacking the Issue

The following manipulative method is seizing the issue. This happens when you raise a point that challenges somebody, and he takes it thinking about something irrelevant to occupy you so you won't define that limit or safeguard that limit.

For instance, suppose it's late, around evening time, and your companion hasn't returned home from work. They haven't called, and you are genuinely stressed because you have no clue about where they are or if something has happened to them. They at last return home, and you face them with how stressed you were and ask them where they were and for what reason they didn't call you to tell you that they would be late.

Maybe then answer your anxiety and questions, they go thinking about something irrelevant about how focused they are busy working and how you're not simply getting it. They may begin to blow up and blame you for having no compassion toward them. You, at that point, end up on the edge side of the conversation and even apologize to them. Presently you're done with the first subject—how late they were and why they didn't call—however, talking about them and what's disturbing them. Eventually, they will try not to respond to your inquiry through and through.

They have seized the conversation and turned it an alternate way. You will regularly wind up sitting them down and saying 'sorry' to them and feeling like you shouldn't trouble them with your minor concerns.

Individuals who utilize these control strategies are not doing as such in a cognizant manner. They're not doing this deliberately. So, they are not commandeering a conversation deliberately; however, they are doing it nonetheless. They don't mean to work up to being a furious monster or stomp all over your limits, yet they do.

They do it to control and control you into continually putting them first.

Chapter 2.
How Did It Come to Be the Favorite Tool of Manipulation for a Narcissist?

Gaslighting also occurs in professional work relationships; a manipulative boss can try to change an employee's perceptions and say things to hurt the employee. A worker can try to bring a subordinate or a coworker down with harmful and destructive words.

Gaslighting happens in television commercial advertisements: a product is advertised, and it leaves you with the feeling that something is wrong with your memory or you are going crazy, and the only way out is for you to buy the product and use it. Public figures, who have a cult-like following, might use their leadership status to mislead the public.

So, what does the term gaslighting mean? "Gaslighting" can be thought of as a verb; we can use it to describe an abusive behavior or action.

To be specific, it refers to the behaviors and actions by which a manipulator uses information in such a way as to make a victim question their sanity.

Gaslighting attempts to convince a person of something being true by forcefully asserting it or making up flimsy evidence, blatantly denying that one has said something one has said.

It is manipulating another's physical environment to make the person doubt their perceptions or memories about their physical situation. It is intentionally isolating another person from external sources of valid information.

You might come to ask at this point how gaslighting became a favorite tool for narcissists; gaslighting can be intentional sometimes, making someone doubt their memories or perception of reality, to defer to the abuser's account of what truth is. It can be used intentionally to gain authority over a victim's life. Narcissists are known as control freaks, and gaslighting is of no surprise a tool they use in controlling the lives of others. A narcissist is anyone who suffers from Narcissism Personality Disorder (NPD). The cause of this disorder is not known, but psychologists link NPD to the environment, genetics, and neurobiology.

It is essential to understand the behaviors of individuals who suffer from NPD because, most times, we don't know what a narcissist looks like. The behaviors of these individuals point them out as narcissists. A narcissist can be said to be someone who exhibits more than one of the following behaviors:

Constant Need for Attention and Validation

Someone who shows a continuous need for attention might be a narcissist; it might be by physically being all over you or constantly saying words to demand your attention. Narcissists can't self-validate, and so they continuously look for other people to approve of them, and no matter what others say to validate them, they never feel it is enough and will always want more. No matter how much you say "I love you" or "I admire you" to a narcissist, they never feel it is enough. They continually attempt to evoke recognition and endorsement from others to support their delicate self-image, but they always need more regardless of their given amount.

Demand for Control All the Time

Narcissists will demand that you say and do precisely what they have in mind so that they can achieve their ideal goals. A narcissist sees you internally as a character in their own script, not a genuine individual with your thoughts and sentiments.

When you don't behave as a narcissist expects you to behave, they become very disturbed because they don't know what to expect from you next as you are now operating outside of their scripts.

The need for control stems out of the narcissist's ideals. Narcissists don't want to believe life is imperfect, and they want to control and mold life into what they envision, so they always want to be in control of everything.

Entitlement

The narcissist sees themselves at the top of the world with everyone beneath their feet. In their heads, they are entitled to the best, and they have to be the best, the richest, the greatest, and so on.

By being entitled, they don't see the world for what it is; they see the world in binary, either good or bad, and they are either superior or inferior beings.

They feel everything must be done their way, and they must own and control everyone.

Refusing Responsibility

At the point when things don't go as planned, the narcissist puts all the fault on others. It must always be another person's deficiency and not theirs. To keep up the façade of flawlessness, narcissists consistently need to accuse some other person or a thing.

Absence of Empathy

Narcissists have next to no capacity to empathize with others. They are too self-absorbed to comprehend what other individuals are feeling. They are also rarely apologetic, remorseful, or guilty.

Narcissists likewise come up short on a comprehension of the idea of emotions. They don't see how their feelings happen. They think their emotions are brought about by a person or thing outside of themselves. They don't understand that their emotions are brought about by their very own natural chemistry and thought patterns. This absence of sympathy makes genuine relationships with narcissists very difficult. They simply don't see what any other individuals are feeling.

Invulnerability

Narcissists are quick to jump from one relationship to another because they desperately want someone to identify with them and feel their pains but are unwilling to respond to the other person's feelings.

The reason for this is that it takes a little vulnerability to keep relationships. Relationships are all about caring and sharing; because of the narcissist's inability to understand feelings, lack of empathy, and constant need for self-security, narcissists can't genuinely love or connect emotionally with other people. They cannot see the world from anyone else's perspective.

Inability to Work as Part of a Team

Being insightful and cooperating with other people requires a genuine comprehension of others' feelings. A narcissist can't genuinely understand other peoples' feelings and won't give up anything for the benefit of others.

Narcissists are also compulsive liars who will go to great lengths to gain power and control over others. The willingness to do anything just to control the actions of others makes gaslighting easy for them to use, and since gaslighting is lying with a goal, the goal of the narcissist is to gain control over the action of another.

Narcissists will use shame and confusion to isolate victims. The narcissist's goal is often to make the target entirely dependent on them alone, and in a bid to control the victim, they will incite fear with words and actions that will make the victim withdraw from loved ones. This withdrawal from loved ones makes it easy for narcissists to abuse victims even more as there are no persons of the third party present to rescue the victims.

Narcissists have a compulsive need to be perfect people at all times, so gaslighting comes in handy in making other peoples' perceptions of an event a wrong one and to show and convince that they are right at all times.

In going to great lengths and doing anything to get their object of desire, narcissists often step on others. Moreover, when they are confronted for their misdoings, they resolve to minimize or erase what they have done and won't hesitate to abuse people to get to this end, making people think how they feel about having their toes stepped on totally unimportant.

This is another form of abuse in itself, as narcissists may use gaslighting to fabricate conversations and events that never happened.

Healthy people display noble acts of selflessness from time to time, but since the world revolves around narcissists, they are always about their feelings and needs, so they employ tactics to dismiss the feelings and needs of others.

Narcissists also love to evade responsibility, and they renege on agreements or promises they have formerly made.

Master manipulators like narcissists can play on people's emotions; they play the victim to evoke sympathy, love, and support for themselves from others. They won't hesitate to use gaslighting to present themselves as persons in pain to sap the feelings of others. Gaslighting overtime effectively disconnects the victim from themselves, their feelings, and their ability to decide and know what they want for themselves.

As gaslighting progress, the victim of abuse will second-guess their thoughts often. Their thought doubting may put them on the defensive and prevent them from criticizing the narcissist's behavior. This self-doubt can give the narcissist more opportunities to manipulate the victim.

Eventually, gaslighting strips the victim of self-identity, the very core of the victim, and leaves them feeling dependent on the narcissist, so the narcissist takes control of their lives and provides approval for them about what reality is.

It doesn't matter whether it's happening in a marriage, or at work, or somewhere else; it is vital to be aware of the signs that you (or someone you know) might be a victim. This awareness is the first step to getting out of this abusive situation.

Gaslighting can cause long-term negative effects on the victim's psychological health, and it takes specialized help to restore the victim's balanced sense of self. Gaslighting only works when the victims are unaware of what is happening, but they can take proactive steps to produce lasting changes once they catch it.

It is essential to realize that anyone and any relationship can be a victim of gaslighting, though it is easier to notice gaslighting in romantic relationships because the end goal is often to gain control. In the end, narcissists often get what they want, and in relating with people at work or in the community, it might be hard to detect gaslighting because, for the most part, in these situations, the goal might not only be in control, it might be other things, money as an example.

The adverse effects of gaslighting can linger on in the victim's mind for a long time, but it is possible to recognize gaslighting at an early stage and avoid the consequences of this form of abuse.

Types of gaslighting!

COUNTERING	WITHHOLDING	TRIVIALIZING	DENIAL	DIVERTING	STEREOTYPING
Question Your Memory	Refusing to Engage in Conversation	Belittling your feelings or disregarding them	Denying something occurred or pretends to forget events	Changes the focus of a discussion and questions your credibility	Using negative stereotypes of a person's gender, race, ethnicity, sexuality, nationality, or age to manipulate them
They may say things such as, "you never remember things accurately," or "are you sure? You have a bad memory."	They may pretend not to understand someone so that they do not have to respond to them. "I do not know what you are talking about," or "you are just trying to confuse me."	They may accuse you of being over-sensitive or overreacting. Their feelings are valid but yours are not. "You are overreacting"	They may accuse you of making it up and deny they ever said something. "I never said that"	They may say something like, "That's just another crazy one of your ideas"	

Chapter 3.
ARE GASLIGHTING AND NARCISSISM THE SAME?

What Is Narcissism?

Narcissism, for lack of a better word, is to be self-obsessed. Someone who has narcissistic tendencies will be self-centered (or, as the saying goes, egotistical). They will do what is in their own best interests and cannot see the greater good or make decisions in the group's interest. For a narcissist, everything is about them.

If you are upset about something that happened at work, they are even more upset about their day, thereby trivializing your experience. If they come to comfort you during your distress, they will do so only because it self-promotes them. People who are narcissists will, for instance, always swing a conversation to be about them.

Gaslighting is a tool that the narcissist uses quite often to manipulate people into a hero-worshipping them. In faking empathy with your suffering, they can dictate your dependence on them as their shoulder to cry on. Without you, the victim, realizing it, the focus has moved away from your suffering to stroking the narcissist's ego. Again, there are different degrees of narcissism, ranging from a severe narcissistic personality disorder (NPD) to milder narcissistic tendencies or an overactive need for attention. It can be emotionally distressing and even abusive when you fall victim to a narcissist's self-centeredness or manipulations. The main difference between this kind of abuse and that caused by gaslighting is that you know it is happening. With gaslighting, you think that the abuse is your idea or that you deserve it. In fact, with gaslighting, you may not even believe that there is abuse happening because the other person (abuser) is your friend and is looking out for you and being supportive.

Whether the person you are being emotionally abused by is a narcissist or they are busy gaslighting you, the results are often the same. Your sense of self takes a pounding, and you end up feeling like you are no good and that there is no one out there who understands you or will help you. With gaslighting, you feel that you are imagining the abuse—perhaps it is not abuse, but just the way that you are (or so the gaslighter has convinced you to think). In examining some of the characteristics of a narcissist and a gaslighter, we can begin to formulate strategies to avoid being manipulated and safeguard our own sense of self.

Characteristics of a Narcissist

There is a range of characteristics and symptoms that are associated with narcissism. These may not always be obvious to spot in our social, family, and work interactions; however, we can spot these characteristics when closely examined. Again, the symptoms of narcissism range in severity to include those who are so self-obsessed that they would even kill someone else to boost their sense of self-achievement at the upper spectrum, right down to your partner being a little obsessed with his body-builder image.

Here are some of the characteristics (according to Mayoclinic.org, n.d.) of narcissism:

Characteristic	Example
An exaggerated sense of self-importance.	A wife who believes her husband was nothing before they got married and that she elevated him.
Belief in entitlement and need for flattery.	A student who believes that the teacher must pay special attention to them since they are so

	incredible. The student then does things to get praised, such as bringing the teacher gifts or showing off their classwork.
Expect to be treated as superior, even when they are not.	A boyfriend who constantly needs his girlfriend to say that he's the best, even though he doesn't really measure up to her past boyfriends.
Exaggerates and even lies about achievements and talents.	We've all met that person who insists on telling you about all their past achievements (president of the youth club, captain of the football team, and head of the cheerleader squad) when, in reality, they didn't excel at or even participate in those events.
Believe that they are superior, and they can only associate with people who are worthy of their presence.	A girl who will not even look at a boy from a different social class to hers and will probably tease him and tear him down to prove her superiority.
Dominate conversations and belittle other people to boost their own sense of self.	That colleague who has to be heard at work. They loudly deliberate the failures of other people to make themselves seem better. Having a "holier than thou" attitude.
Expect special favors and compliance with their demands.	A husband who dictates what is to be cooked for supper while he contributes little to the household.
Unable or unwilling to value the feelings or needs of others.	You tell a "friend" that you had a terrible day at work or a family crisis, and this person proceeds to trivialize your feelings by telling

	you that their day was even worse (as a competition) or they tell you that their day was brilliant (since they're so fabulous).
Arrogant, boastful, and pretentious	In our social and work interactions, we often find that one person who has to tell you (and everyone) how incredible they are. They attended the best schools (even though the schools were average), they achieved the best results (even though they didn't), and they know exactly what to do (even though they didn't have a clue).
Envy and praise.	A father who is jealous of the other dads at his kid's school while demanding that his child constantly tells everyone that he has the best dad in the world.

Apart from these 10 characteristics, the habits of narcissists include: not caring about others and bullying others into doing as the narcissist wants. Narcissists are often drawn to other narcissists since there is an image of perfection that they create, which will appeal to the other party. Narcissists are excellent pretenders.

They score well in interviews where they can usually convince their victims (or subjects) of their excellent personalities. Lastly, narcissists are defensive by nature.

They will argue when their flaws are pointed out and can even become aggressive if they feel that their perfect self-image is being threatened (Mayoclinic.org, n.d.).

Are Gaslighting and Narcissism the Same?

Though gaslighting and narcissism may not always be the same, gaslighters are usually narcissistic in nature since they use their manipulations to build their power base. It allows them to feel superior toward their victims. Narcissists may use gaslighting as a tool to reach their goals or simply engage in it when the occasion arises. Some narcissists are too self-absorbed to turn to gaslight, or they lack the basic empathy to even begin manipulating their victims. However, the two conditions do share some characteristics such as:

Characteristic Shared	How Both Narcissists and Gaslighters Reflect This
Entitlement beliefs	Both narcissists and gaslighters believe that it is their right to behave a certain way towards others.
Exaggerates and lies	Both parties will engage in exaggeration ("You're being paranoid" or "I am the best husband") or lying ("You are not thinking rationally").
Unwilling to value the emotions of others	Narcissists will undercut the feelings of others ("Stop being a baby") and not value or validate the feelings of others ("You don't deserve that promotion, but congratulations").
Arrogance and manipulation	Gaslighters and narcissists both believe in their right to act the way that they do. They have a deep arrogance, and this feeds their entitlement issues.

By looking at the nature of narcissists, we can gain further insight into gaslighting and why people do it and determine the signs of manipulation and abuse.

Chapter 4.
BASICS AND TYPES OF NARCISSISTIC ABUSE

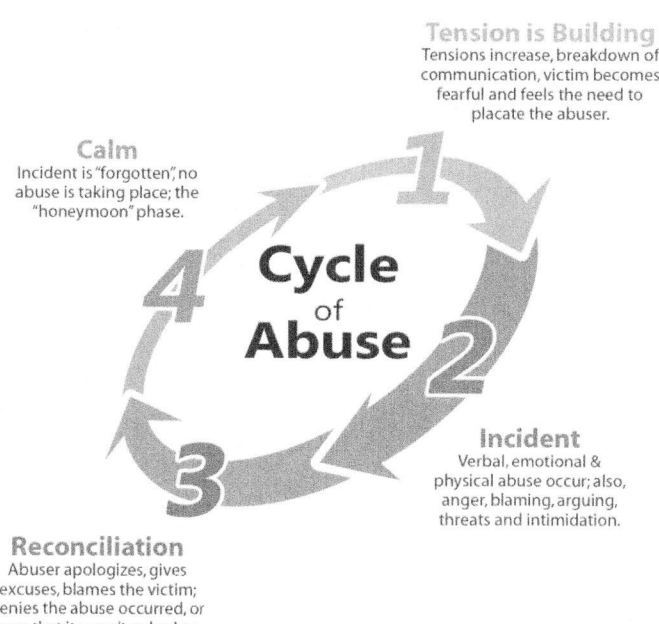

We may describe narcissism as a mental inclination to get acclaim from others as detailed positive or backhanded appraisals, with a particularly steady treatment, joined with reverence.

Besides, narcissistic individuals are recognized by fulfilling certain attributes in accordance with the far-reaching confidence:

considerations of prevalence for themselves, inclination to disparage specific individuals, and trouble in sympathizing, different things.

It is a mental quality that can be seen in shifting degrees of seriousness. The more extreme it is, the more likely it will be categorized as a dysfunctional behavior side effect class. Anyway, not all individuals with high narcissism have a psychological issue that extraordinarily harms their personal satisfaction.

Be that as it may, similarly as we can see varieties in the degrees of seriousness of this state of mind, certain subjective types can likewise be recognized in how narcissism is passed on.

In particular, Dr. Bruce Stevens gives a meaning of narcissism styles that can assist us with seeing all the complexities of this character quality.

Narcissistic Emotional Dependent

This sort of narcissism is set apart by outrageous "weakness." This narcissistic individual encounters a colossal requirement for adoration, which nothing fulfills. It resembles a pit without a base that never fills. They simply accept they don't get enough love; they feel briefly happy with others' consideration, yet then they experience that void of endorsement and fondness once more.

A profound dread of dismissal and relinquishment is at the premise of this conduct, so the narcissist sticks to reliance. They have no apprehensions about controlling others to address those issues. Their enthusiastic requests are rising, so their accomplices and close individuals are depleting sincerely to attempt to support, comfort, and continue that "I" that needs fondness.

Narcissistic Tyrant

This narcissist sticks to control since they have a voracious requirement for power and strength. This individual is haughtily acting, thinking they are predominant, once in a while scorning others and regarding them like they were "second rate." They think they are in every case right and should be in charge of the circumstance, so frequently, their simple nearness is abusive.

At the point when such a narcissist takes power, they make life exceptionally hard for their subordinates. They use it as a Trophy while they are seeing someone. They article to individuals by and large, who are simply a method for exhibiting their capacity and satisfying their requirement for power. To the point of misuse, this narcissistic individual is exceptionally possessive. However, they have no disgrace in utilizing disregard to cause others to feel like failures, demonstrating that they're a champ.

Elitist Narcissistic

This kind of narcissism is portrayed by an overstated impression of the "I." Here, the narcissist accepts they are the most remarkable, influential, and notable individual on the planet. To ensure that others know and bow to them, they generally trumpet their alleged victories and achievements. They, by and large, misrepresent its significance since they need to stir jealousy or adoration.

This individual consistently offers their input, in any event, when they don't request it, and accepts that they know more than anybody, paying little heed to the current point. They regularly believe that they are bound to accomplish incredible things and that they merit extraordinary things, regardless of whether they don't do anything to accomplish them. They can regularly be an alluring individual, which is the reason they can draw in numerous admirers to their "circle," who at last wind up understanding that "it is a ton of commotion and not many nuts."

Fantasy Narcissistic

This narcissistic individual grows incredibly complex dreams to the degree that nearly their entire life is committed to their inward world. They think this present reality is included; accordingly, they feel outraged and disappointed in their optimal world. They consider life to be cold and hard, so they attempt to disregard it and just look for satisfaction in the ideal world, where they are an ideal person, have a perfect profession, and are all around associated.

On the off chance that this individual converse with others, they guarantee it is substantial in their own universe, so they lie over and over. The jealousy and appreciation of others are likewise created into an anecdotal reality. Furthermore, regardless of whether they are confronting reality, they despise everything to look for motivation to support their minds. They frequently don't recall their untruths.

Somatic Narcissistic

Looking great or sound is imperative to wellbeing; however, the narcissism of this sort goes above and beyond, as a fixation on the body and appearance is included. Picture, style, tastefulness, youth, and excitement are the estimations of this human. They should be lauded in light of the fact that they have an inseparably associated confidence with their self-perception.

This individual is an ordinarily very stickler and invests a lot of energy in their body care and excellence ceremonies. The issue is that they stretch out this conduct to others and judge them as per their body size. They additionally feel that their looks and wellbeing are what they merit.

Narcissistic Antagonist

This is one of the most well-known types of narcissism, the disappointment of which is under the surface. Here, the dissatisfaction of an individual is reflected in heightened enmity to everything. There's consistently a foe who will hurt this narcissistic person. They likewise experience "nonsensical," baffling, or strange triggers in dangerous fierceness. It is typically physical hostility that "wipes" individuals around them and damages them.

Having touchiness behind this conduct, they can't see any word as an affront or irreverence for its significance if the individual doesn't get the commendation and adoration they sought. They accept everything as a personal attack, which triggers their fierceness. The "I" is viewed as a narcissistic physical issue.

Narcissist Trickster

The individual endeavors to show their best face in this type of narcissism. They're sweet and benevolent, in any event at the beginning. This intrigue is, unfortunately, only a stain that covers a darker figure. There are vindictive aims behind the "trust me" post.

The narcissist looks for, actually, to win the trust of others in support of themselves. They play out a sort of "enthusiastic defacement," the mischief of which is extreme to the point that casualties frequently have quite a long while to recuperate and confide in someone else. This narcissist utilizes their allure to grin and loots others.

Narcissistic Martyr

This is one of the most troublesome types of narcissism to distinguish because it centers around anguish. The narcissist's very own recognizable proof is centered on misery, victimhood, or even survivorship. The requirement for consideration and parasite necessities, which lead to lopsided and exploitative connections, pardons languishing.

This individual clearly conveys enormous, passionate gear.

There will never be the agony of the past. They sully the present with the enduring that makes them a remarkable individual in their psyche. It tends to be hard to talk about these narcissists since they never address our issues for help, but since no one is truly harming, they don't have a difficult time; they consistently request backing and consideration. On the off chance that this exposure is declined to them, they don't spare a moment to censure themselves for making a feeling of regret that empowers them to claim to be a saint.

Messianic Narcissistic

Such narcissism appears by individuals who consider themselves to be more significant, better, and more neighborly than others, thus looking on others and judging them over their shoulders. You believe you're a sort of Messiah.

They don't spare a moment to list all their otherworldly "encounters" to be commended by others. They are a legend, yet their evidently uninvolved help brings different conditions. They don't stop for a second to attest favors and demand that their supposed "penance" is constantly maintained, so the association turns into a lasting obligation.

Vengeful Narcissism

This is one of the most hazardous narcissistic structures. This individual generally works out of the shadows, utilizing duplicity to slaughter individuals. This individual needs to annihilate others so as to feel unrivaled. Along these lines, they don't have any outrage over contradictions or the creation of falsehoods that influence their rivals. For whatever length of time that their "foes" break down, they can do nearly nothing.

This narcissist experiences Procusto Syndrome. As opposed to trying to create and transform, they dismiss somebody who exceeds expectations and endeavors to get them up and stigmatize them to wreck their notoriety. They might be the object of recognition and thankfulness thusly.

Tactics Narcissists Will Use to Manipulate You

At the point when you're a child and learn somebody is narcissistic, you would already be able to picture an individual glancing in the mirror throughout the day. An individual who thinks they beautiful love their own picture. While contorting our feeling of confidence completely (on the off chance that you view yourself as alluring is to be narcissistic, consequently, be humble), it likewise makes us disregard something significant: Narcissism is far more noteworthy and can cause us much harm.

There are numerous attributes of a narcissist, yet the essential one is self-centeredness. Also, it's not simply the narrow-mindedness of not obtaining a metallic-hued pencil from Faber Castell, no. The narrow-mindedness is one that the individual wishes just themselves the best. The prideful individual can't wish the best for other people. Think about the poop, which is a relationship with an individual like that.

However, unfortunately, these connections are ordinary, as narcissists have effective manipulative ways.

In this way, to abstain from getting into such connections, in the case of cherishing, friendly, or even proficient, it's significant for us to know how the narcissists' key controls work.

Triangulation

At the point when you wouldn't dare to hope anymore, they are embedded in a triangle. It's not tied in with cheating, and it's about continually including others in your horse crap. By one way or another, the narcissist consistently gets somebody to support them and guarantee that you are incorrect.

Do you realize that the "I conversed with my mother, and she said no doubt about it" thing?

So…

Devaluation

Sooner or later, you were everything the narcissist needed. Unexpectedly, it appears to be that every little thing about you is aggravating and disdainful; nothing you do is correct.

This is an approach to cause you to accept that you have to work considerably more complex to satisfy yourself.

Aggression

As indicated by some social exploration, narcissists are exceptionally joined to a forceful character, both physical and verbal, notwithstanding being not able to control their upheavals. Physical assaults are anything but difficult to distinguish, while mental assaults can happen for quite a long time without the casualty monitoring it.

As indicated by the National Domestic Violence Hotline, these are the attributes of a mental victimizer:

- They make you feel afraid in some way;
- They threaten you;
- They use derogatory language;
- They deny emotional, physical, or financial support;
- They control your contact with friends and family;
- They control their behavior;
- They pressure you to do things you don't want to do.

Decrease

To deprecate individuals and attempt to lessen them is a type of control, in the event that the narcissist figures out how to humiliate you by your appearance, training, or social class, they will feel better by examination.

Playing the Victim

At the point when a controller understands that their strategies have fizzled, they advance to their sympathy. This frequently incorporates attempting to legitimize their swelled personality by accusing your activities. Try not to get bulldozed.

Inappropriate Behavior

Have you at any point needed to apologize for another person's conduct? Thus, you've been controlled! A narcissist can openly act in an overstated manner, maltreating sexual words and terms and irritating people around them.

Trust me; saying 'sorry' to them just makes them consider you to be somebody who will tidy up the jumble, and when they need to, they can act like a moron.

Conversation Monopoly

Everything is about them, so don't be shocked if a narcissist isn't giving any consideration to what exactly you're deliberating. Besides, they generally will, in general, take the conversation back to themselves and intrude on a ton, yet they don't endure being hindered in any capacity.

Narcissists HATE being interfered with.

Projection

Attempt to blame a narcissist for something incorrectly; they will accuse the conduct of you, in light of the fact that, obviously, they are immaculate.

Brainwashing

Have you at any point wound up accomplishing something you would not like to manage without knowing why? Almost certainly, you have been controlled. By one way or another, narcissists figure out how to persuade you to get things done without wanting to.

Gaslighting

Okay, an old associate's gaslighting is an apparatus generally utilized by mental cases, sociopaths, and ... NARCISSISTS. One of the most exceedingly awful sorts of control makes you question your own mental stability. They will deny something that truly occurred until you begin to dishonor your head. At long last, you trust you envision things.

Verbal Aggression

Yells and put-down are other types of control. The goal is to cause you to feel little and apprehensive. Remain quiet, keep your manner of speaking, and request that the narcissist does likewise. On the off chance that it doesn't work, decline to talk at that point.

Chapter 5.

ACKNOWLEDGING ABUSE AND RECOVERY RECOMMENDED ACTIVITIES

No matter the improvements you notice in your self-esteem by applying the suggestions, it is almost impossible to completely free yourself from the negative impacts of Gaslighting as long as you continue to engage the Gaslighter. If a gaslighter is willing to take steps toward seeking help from an expert, it may be worth giving them the benefit of the doubt. Notice that I said if the Gaslighter seeks help from an expert. One mistake common to victims of Gaslighting is trying to play the role of an expert therapist. You are not a therapist; you can't change anyone (even therapists don't change anyone), so don't even attempt to change anyone.

However, it is rarely the case to have Gaslighters seeking help, especially in romantic relationships. Many Gaslighters are mischievous Narcissists with sick minds and can hardly recognize anything wrong with their behaviors. This is why your best option is to end your relationship with a Gaslighter and don't ever look back.

If you must regain control of your life, trust your judgment, become psychologically and emotionally balanced again, then you must cut off any contact with Gaslighters. You must completely dissociate from people who make you doubt your instincts and judgments. You must consciously create an environment that supports that "inner knowing" where you just feel something is off without anyone making you think that you are crazy, too sensitive, or overreacting.

Taking steps to rebuild your self-esteem and recognizing your true self-worth is important. It is equally vital to engage in practices that can help you piece your life together again. Regardless of how silly they may appear to you at first, you will be more equipped to protect yourself from Gaslighters and other emotional abusers with constant practice.

Your Inner Talk

There is a massive difference between leaving an abusive relationship and healing or recovery. Cutting all ties with a Gaslighter is like removing a piece of clothing. You're not going to walk around naked, just like you're not likely to stop relating to every other person. You need to put on another piece of clothing; you have to connect with other people. But if you don't make inner changes, you can still inadvertently get into another abusive relationship or partnership. Stop expecting others to change for you to have a better relationship. The changes must begin from you—deep within you. For this reason, you must make concerted efforts to change your inner self-talk. Consider using the following exercises.

Thought-Awareness Exercise

Most times, our thoughts are on auto-pilot, and this is mostly a good thing. It will be unrealistic and unhelpful to try to monitor every thought you have because that is impossible and more than a full-time job! However, if most of your thoughts are negative or self-sabotaging, having those thoughts on auto-pilot will harm you more than good.

Living or associating with a Gaslighter for long can make your thoughts predominantly negative, especially thoughts about yourself. To make matters worse, if you have endured a gaslighter for a long time, you have likely habituated these patterns of thoughts that almost feel normal. But you can change all that, beginning right now.

Deliberately take several pauses during your day to notice the contents of your thoughts. Mentally take note of what you are thinking about yourself or write down your thoughts if you prefer.

Observe the thought without criticism or judgment. Simply notice the idea irrespective of how it makes you feel—good or bad.

Now, write down a short statement that describes the thought. For example, "I am thinking of how stupid everyone will think I am if I tell them how I feel."

The next step is to challenge or question that line of thinking by writing down several statements that will dislodge the negative thought. In the preceding example, you could write challenging reports such as, "Really? Everyone will think I am stupid? How do I know that?" And "I've got some great friends and loved ones who understand and support me. They'll tell me if they think I am making a mistake, but they definitely won't think I am stupid." Continue to add as many affirmative statements to reinforce positive thoughts and diminish any negative thoughts and perceptions you have about yourself.

Repeat this as often as you can to help you habituate a different thought pattern. This way, your auto-pilot thoughts will begin to serve you better.

Self-Interview Exercise

Have you ever been in a hot seat? Have you watched a show where someone was in a hot seat? Well, this exercise puts you in the hot seat with an interviewer. But in this case, you are both the interviewer and the interviewee. So, you will be answering questions from no one but you. To help you remember the self-interview exercise, set timers that will go off at different times a day. The duration for this exercise is entirely up to you, but I recommend doing this exercise at least twice daily for a minimum of five minutes. (You eat at least three times a day, right?)

Here are some questions to ask yourself during the interview:
- What have I been telling myself in the last 30 minutes?
- What has been the tone of my inner monologue for the last 30 minutes? Have I been talking to myself kindly, reassuringly, supportively, or have I been overly harsh and demeaning? Would I talk to my best friend using the same tone?
- What has been my emotional state for the past 30 minutes? Have I been feeling anxious, stressed, or relaxed?
- What are the things I've been telling myself in this emotional state? Do I tend to bash myself when I'm in a tense state, or do I offer reassurance?

What believable thing can I honestly say to myself right now to make me feel better? Note that telling yourself positive-sounding words doesn't necessarily make you feel better. Your goal should be a gradual shift from negative to positive and not a quantum leap from feeling despair, for example, to feeling exhilaration. Such jumps are not sustainable.

Mirror Work

Mirror work (not to be confused with shadow work) is a powerful exercise designed to reconnect you with your core self and rebuild your self-esteem. Gaslighting may push you to begin to think that your world is falling apart. Mirror work can correct that impression to make you begin to see a meaningful world around you again.

Victims of Gaslighting have a difficult time being intimate not just with others but with themselves because the Gaslighter has eroded their self-confidence. The mirror work puts you in touch with yourself again by making you stare at your reflection in the mirror. This can be an unsettling experience for many people because it can bring up harsh criticism at first. But no one can ever truly become free of their past without confronting it. If you shudder in fear of your past, you are still enslaved by it.

To practice the mirror work, you will need to:

- Do the practice for at least five minutes each day in front of a mirror.
- Use a private space where you will not be disturbed throughout your exercise.
- Create meaningful, believable, and positive affirmations that apply to you directly. Vague or general affirmations can be a great waste of your time and effort, no matter how positive they sound. You can say things such as, "I believe in myself," "I trust my intuition," "I am wise," and "I trust my abilities." Make them short, powerful, and believable. Don't include words such as can't, don't, not, won't, and other terms that negate in your affirmations. Instead of saying, "I

am not weak," or "I won't give up," say, "I am strong," or "I am steadfast."

- Allow yourself to feel the emotions that come up during the exercise. Don't fight or suppress any feelings that come to the surface.
- Keep a record of your progress in a journal.

The process is as follows:

Stand in front of a mirror (your dressing mirror or bathroom mirror will work just fine).

Maintain eye contact with yourself for at least five minutes. It is okay to blink, but continue to look at yourself for the duration of the practice. You may feel uneasy, embarrassed, awkward, or emotional during this process, and that is okay. Just lock eyes with your reflection and allow yourself to take in all the emotions.

Repeat your personalized affirmations while staring directly into your eyes.

This can help to reprogram your self-talk. This exercise can reconnect you to your inner child and shift your perspective to one of innocent and empowerment.

Shift Your Self-Perception

You are not a loser, even if Gaslighters want you to believe otherwise. The following suggestions can help you change the way you see yourself from a weak, fearful, and powerless person to an empowered, strong, and self-confident person.

Do Something Off-Limits

Gaslighters will make you believe that you can't do something, are not good at something, or are incapable of comprehending anything meaningful. But that is all part of their lies.

Whether it is a hobby, career, or an experience you've always wished to explore, go right ahead and do it.

Begin to break all limits (real or perceived) that Gaslighters have placed on you.

Step out of your comfort zone and challenge yourself to do the 'unthinkable.'

Remember to start with baby steps. You don't have to do something overwhelming because you want to break free from limitations. Be realistic, but don't forget the role of healthy optimism.

However, one thing you must keep in mind is to do the things you want to do because you truly enjoy doing them.

Doing something because you want to spite a Gaslighter only shows that they still have control over you.

Act out of your conscious free will and not because you have a point to prove or you want someone else to feel bad.

Help Others

This may seem a little bit far-fetched, especially for someone trying to get back on their feet after surviving an emotionally abusive relationship. But helping others, even in small ways, can help to boost the production of oxytocin, dopamine, serotonin, and all the other feel-good hormones in your brain (Psychology Today, 2014). Interestingly, the level of your feel-good hormones is linked to your willingness to help others. In other words, the more feel-good hormones are released in your brain, the more you will want to help other people, and the more you help other people, the more feel-good hormones are released. It is a chain reaction.

Start with small acts of kindness, whatever that would be for you. It will make the beneficiaries of your kindness feel good and also make you feel good. The result is an overall improvement in your self-esteem.

Emulate Habits from Role Models and Mentors

Find people with qualities that you appreciate and emulate them. Learning new positive habits from people who inspire you is a great way to prove to yourself that you can do anything you set your mind to. Also, cultivate the habit of reading positive books and gather as many positive ideas as you can from them. Instead of listening to a Gaslighter, find role models and mentors who will repeat empowering ideas to you over and over to reinforce your belief in yourself.

One More Thing… Be on the Lookout for the "Hoovering" Tactics

Consider these real-world scenarios:

- **Scenario 1**: Owen kept showing up at Olivia's doorstep even after a nasty breakup. Olivia had decided to rid herself of Owen's Gaslighting and take charge of her life. But he was persistent and sounded convincing. He would stand outside her door for hours on end, pleading. One day, Olivia couldn't resist anymore; she yanked her door open and screamed, "Leave me alone! Stay out of my life!" She broke down crying as Owen hugged her and let her cry out, her heart on his shoulder.

- **Scenario 2:** Lucas was feeling lonely after six long months of ending an abusive relationship with his ex-wife. She would call him several times a week in the guise of letting their only child speak with him. Lucas missed his family so much that when his ex-wife apologized for her abusive behavior, he began to consider giving her another chance.

- **Scenario 3:** Paula had ended her relationship with Mike and cut off all contact with him for more than three months. Out of the blue, she got an email from Mike apologizing profusely for all the pain and hurt he had caused her. He told Paula how he couldn't bring himself to love any other woman because he was still in love with her. Paula's heart raced, loving memories flooded her, and she hit the reply button, believing that Mike had turned a new leaf.

Chapter 6.
THE NARCISSIST/GASLIGHTER EXPLORED

So, we mentioned that narcissists have a hand in gaslighting, but what do they do/ they actually are big manipulators, and they play a major role in changing the reality of others. Here, we'll talk about how they gaslight others and why narcissists are bad news for many people.

What Is A Narcissist?

A narcissist is, by definition, someone that has a narcissistic personality disorder. Those who are narcissists tend to have an overly inflated sense of importance and a need for admiration and attention in their relationships and often don't empathize with others.

Narcissists only care about themselves. They don't worry about you or the guy next to you, but instead, they're only in it for their own benefit. However, they actually have an incredibly fragile ego that will shatter and is very vulnerable if they're hit with the smallest amount of criticism.

Narcissists are textbook manipulators, and they're not fun to deal with. This type of personality causes many issues in different areas of life, and you may run into one of these types without even realizing it. Typically, though, those who have narcissistic personality disorder are unhappy in a general sense if they're not given the admiration they want. They may find all of their relationships unfulfilling, and others may not like being around these types of people.

So how does a narcissist come into your life? Well, those that suffer from this love latch onto those that will hype them up, making them feel like they're special or unique, and in turn, enhance their own self-esteem as a result. They may desire an immense amount of admiration and attention and have difficulty taking criticism in the slightest. They oftentimes see all criticism as defeat.

They are incredibly envious of your accomplishments, to the point where they will want to undermine them; however, they can. This can be anything from snarky achievements regarding your success to underhanded comparing of others.

Narcissists love to use gaslighting too, but we'll get to that in a bit. For now, let's talk about how they will undermine you. If you do something great, they'll try to belittle it, saying that it's not worth it, and you need to do better. Sometimes, if the narcissist is a parent, they'll compare you to your sibling or someone else in the family. They frequently will try to belittle anything you do, turning you into a mess in response.

It's not good, and narcissists in general only care about themselves. Of course, many times, only a tiny fraction of people are actual narcissists, but in general, there are more male narcissists than female narcissists, and you oftentimes will run into them when you're dealing with bosses, coworkers, or even people you may be friends with or date.

But, how can these people use gaslighting? Well, they do so in a very crafty manner.

Narcissism and Gaslighting

Narcissists love to use gaslighting. In fact, it's their favorite, most preferred tool of gaslighting. Why is that? Well, it's because it's the perfect way to make you think you're crazy, to undermine what you think is right completely, and to tell you that your way of thinking is wrong, basically.

Remember, gaslighting is a sneaky way of making you feel like your reality is so distorted that the person will question their sanity or even their memory. Their goal is to make it so that they're right, you're wrong, and that's all they want from this.

The goal is to make you think you're crazy, which we'll get to in a bit. There are other tools narcissists will use, but gaslighting is their bread and butter.

"Oh, I never said that."

"Oh, you remember it wrong, clearly you should get yourself checked out."

If you've ever heard those two things before from someone, you're dealing with a Grade A Narcissist.

Narcissists use gaslighting because it's how they love to hide the abuse they're inflicting upon you. In essence, gaslighting is lying straight to your face, with one singular goal in mind, to be the ones in control, the center of attention, and you're nothing.

Basically, every time a narcissist gaslight you, they're wholly ruining what sense of reality you have, making you realize that it's nothing, and they're everything.

They want to break you down slowly but surely. Memory is one of the easiest ways to do this. Why is that? Well, it's because they know that if you can't remember things right, you're not going to be able to trust yourself, distorting your personal perception and reality that comes with this.

So yes, it does happen like that, and the goal is for you to entirely rely on the abuser to tell you what's real so that over time the abuser is the one in control of your life, the one taking the reins here in the game.

The Art of Making Others Crazy

This is something that a lot of narcissists use gaslighting for. Remember, gaslighting is basically refuting anyone's reality, making it so that what they think is right really isn't.

When a narcissist gaslight, they will put down and refute anything that you say. They will do this to make it sound like they're the ones who are right when in reality, it's their own mind games.

It's all a game for a narcissist. They want to make it so that your reality isn't correct. While you might believe that you're right, the narcissist will tell you right away that you aren't. Over time as you continue to be refuted by the narcissist, you start to doubt your own reality. You begin to think that you're the bad guy when in fact, it's just your narcissist playing games.

When a narcissist gaslight, they can change the view you have of people being good in general. You might think that people, in general, are good, which they are, but oftentimes, if you have a narcissist in your life, this person will not protect your feelings. Someone you may think is good turns out to be wrong, and someone that you thought was bad turns out to be good since that's how the narcissist wants you to believe.

A narcissist will use gaslighting for the sole reason of, they know exactly how to manipulate you. You start to doubt your own reality, and over time, you start to wonder if maybe you are crazy. After all, after so often, you may wonder if you're not right in the head. But remember, more often than not, narcissists were the cause of this, and they're the reason why you think this way.

Many times, narcissists will start by buttering you up, making you feel loved and appreciated since that's what they want you to believe. After a while, they will begin to, over time, start to treat you like crap. When you call them out on it, they'll start to mask their true feelings, and you'll be seeing a totally different side.

But the reality is, that mask that they put on is, of course, their mask, and the abusive nature that they've had till now is their proper form. It can slowly erode the trust that you've had in yourself. After all, you thought that you could trust this person to always be there for you, and you start to notice they're nowhere near as good. Up, after a bit, you realize that they're actually garbage, and you begin to see how they really are.

They will tell you what you think is what happened isn't what happened, but that's actually how it is. But of course, in the world of the narcissist, they'll only make you believe what they think is right.

Gaslighting basically takes away everything you think is correct, which causes you to follow what they believe is the way when in reality, they're manipulating you.

You're forced to believe that you're crazy, or if you don't think you're crazy, that the abuser is wrong, but you can't stand up for yourself. They will either manipulate you until you believe you're wrong and they are right or drive you to the point of insanity.

Gaslighters and narcissists love this. Because they know that, once you discount your own personal beliefs enough, you'll start to really think that you are crazy and slowly start to believe them.

Making People do What the Narcissist Wants

This is done because most of the time, when you start to discount how a narcissist acts, they will immediately gaslight you, saying that it didn't happen this way.

You notice your narcissist abuser is acting gross and mean, and you see that they're flirting with other girls. They totally are, and you call them out on it, but they will immediately say that isn't the case, tell you that you're crazy, that you're making stuff up, and basically tell you whatever you saw was wrong.

Deep down, you know what the truth is. The actions you saw were valid, but this person will continuously tell you that you're crazy and didn't really hear or say what was said over time.

You start to doubt your own reality, and you begin to wonder if you remembered everything right. Perhaps you didn't catch the other person flirting with girls.

You start to go silent on it. When in reality, your narcissist was totally doing that, didn't come clean, and now this person is seeing girls, and every time you call them out on that, and their own trust and validity, basically tells you that you're insane, and you're wrong.

You stop fighting the narcissist after a while. You notice that every time you fight them, there really is no end to it, and the fact that you're constantly told that you're crazy every time you do isn't a good thing for you either. So, what do you do from here?

The answer is most people tend to give in to their abusers.

Instead of doing what they feel is right, which is calling out the abuser and recognizing the toxic traits, you start to do exactly what the abuser wants. Because whenever you're gaslit, you start to feel like you're wrong and that the narcissist is right. You're pretty much duped into believing that the narcissist is the right person, and you're wrong, making your reality practically nothing.

If you let this continue, you're basically feeding the supply of narcissism that the other person craves. You may start to perceive things wrong, and oftentimes, it gets to the point where you swore it was that way, but maybe your stuff is gone because the narcissist hides it, and then they claim that you're irresponsible and not worthy of trust. They will then tell you that you're wrong and crazy, and they'll start to make others think that you're crazy.

They will even pit others against you to isolate others. Often, they'll try to put you against others, so you drop them, and the only person in your life is the narcissist. They'll make up lies, and you can't really trust anyone but the person who is gaslighting you.

When in reality, the one who is gaslighting you is the last person you should trust!

Gaslighters don't really realize just how harmful they are, or maybe they do. They will start to make you question even the most random of strangers. You might begin to brush off someone's actions as being harmless, but the gaslighted will call it flirting, and soon, you start to attack anyone who comes at you.

Have you ever seen this? Maybe you've experienced it. Where you will hear about how someone was looking at you the wrong way, you start to grow weary and angry with the other person, and over time, those relationships break down since you think they can't be trusted. When in reality, it's the narcissist who can't be charged because they're the one putting you in this direction.

A narcissist will hurt everyone in your life literally, pit you against the friends and family you have so that you're distracted from what the narcissist is really doing, which feeds you harmful lies.

It's a messy situation and not something that most of us want to deal with.

So yes, a narcissist will use gaslighting. It's the prime tool of narcissists because they know that they can bend others to the will that they have, making it very easy to manipulate them, and that's why many narcissists will smile at you with a warm, fake smile and then stab you in the back whenever you turn around or put your family and friends against you, so the only person you can really rely on, is the narcissist themselves

Chapter 7.
Signs of Emotional Abuse

When left to thrive in a relationship, gaslighting portends doom for its victims. It can affect their emotional, psychological, physical, and spiritual well-being. Spotting this malaise from the onset and shutting it down will minimize its adverse impacts in our lives in the long run.

So, how do you know that you are being gaslighted?
The following signs can provide a clue:

When You are Habitually Lied To

In my college days, I had this excellent friend of mine, Vicka. We were best of friends and held no secret from each other. We were always deliberating our plans with each other, talking about our current relationships, the boys, fashion trends, and other such mundane things young girls talk about. Vicka was a pretty lady in her early twenties, very smart and easy-going. She was able to make friends with people easily and turned every social event into a chance to meet someone new. She was very extroverted and had a vivacious personality. She met this charming medical student in one of the campus parties she attended and was swept off her feet by his charm and gentle mien. I, for one, thought he meant well for her, as he exuded this "can't hurt a fly" personality. He was unusually quiet, very charming, and soft-spoken. One of the reasons Vicka caught the love bug. A relationship soon commenced between them, and it seemed a match made in heaven.

There was a period of bliss between them, the calm before the storm. Then came the downward spiral. He was a serial cheat and a liar who lied even in the slightest, unnecessary things. When confronted over his cheating habits, he would lie outrightly and turned the whole affair against Vicka. The evidence was there—the ladies' stuff all over his apartment, his disappearance for weeks on end, the calls he had to hide before he could take, the number of ladies that flocked to his apartment, even the way, and manner he flirted with close friends of Vicka. All these he dismissed with a wave of the hand.

On his birthday, though out of town, she decided to pay him a surprise visit. He got angry about why she should arrive unannounced and wouldn't let her in. She forced her way in and could see a lady hurriedly leaving through the back door. This he blatantly denied also. And was pretty angry; she could even suggest she saw a lady in his apartment. He questioned the quality of her eyesight (she was actually shortsighted and wore glasses). He called her delusional and accused her of seeing things that were not there.

Was her mind playing tricks on her? "Maybe I really didn't see a lady in there." She told herself, "Maybe the make-up kits in his bathroom are his sister's," even when she knew he got no female siblings.
She repeatedly questioned her sanity. She made excuses for his many failings and tried to reconcile his lies with her own perceptions.
That, right there, is the gaslighting effect in action.

Gaslighters, when caught even red-handed, would look you right in the eye and tell you nothing of such occurred. You begin to question your sense of reality—"is my mind playing tricks on me?" Gaslighters want you to believe only their own version of events. Everything you say does not matter; only theirs does.
They are habitual liars who would, over time, come to believe their own lies. When with a gaslighting partner, they refuse to believe their own version of events when all facts they put out point to the contrary.

When You Start Withholding Information from Friends and Family

Vicka was one person who had never withheld information from me in the past. We knew each other's secrets. We knew what was going on in each other's life at every given time. This was also extended to our different families, as our parents sometimes called either of us to get a clue on what the other party would like as a present on any memorable occasion. The bond was that strong. Not until Mr. Charming came into the picture. Vicka wouldn't let me on whatever was happening in her life anymore. I lost count of the many times I had to lie to her family just to get her off some really tight situation. I was now the outsider. Mr. Charming became the new go-to person for every kind of need. Evidently, my bestie was a victim of the gaslighting effect.

She withheld information from her family members and me, so she wouldn't have to explain off certain things going wrong in her relationship.

They Compare You to Others

Gradually he began to compare her to his past girlfriends. He once told her point blank that she was fat and would have to lose weight rapidly, or he would look elsewhere. This was someone that had before chided her on how skinny she looked. She religiously took to regimented eating and workout programs. Fortunately, her discipline paid off, and she lost some weight. She now had this killer figure most ladies could kill for. Yet, Mr. Charming wasn't satisfied.

She was left confused and in a state of hysteria. Where was this coming from? Why the sudden change of heart? This is the gaslighter's stock-in-trade. It is a control tool for them.

Thus, with a gaslighter, you can never win their outright approval. For them, perfection is unattainable, and no matter how hard you try to meet their expectations, you will always fall short. So don't try to, to begin with.

You Constantly second-guess Yourself

When it gets to that point where you now have to think through your every move or evaluate past decisions on the basis of whether he would like it or not, then you are neck-deep in the gaslighting effect. Being the lively and chatty type, Vicka would always want to engage and talk with people she had just met. This usually gets Mr. Charming pretty upset, and he would accuse her of flirting with every guy she meets and rubbing it in his face. To win his much-needed approval, she retreated into her shell and stopped being that life-of-the-party she was.

And that's the horror victims of gaslighting undergoes.

They lose their identity. They lose themselves trying to bend to the will of their gaslighters.

Instead of seeing him for who he was—The jealous, insecure boyfriend, she makes excuses for his behavior. "I'm truly flirting with guys I just met and would have to stop." He twisted every innocent action of hers into something meant to hurt him. "You allowed that friend of yours to take you to lunch.

Don't you see how you're hurting my feelings?" She was trapped. A simple explanation will not do. She now has to evaluate every move before she makes them in the guise of just being careful.

You Have a Sense of Becoming a Totally Different Person

You now have this constant feeling of being a different person. You know this is just not you. You know someone else with a totally new worldview. What changed? You can't place your fingers on it. You just know you weren't like this.

When Friends Try Saving You from Yourself

Your friends have noticed the rapid changes in you. You just can't see it clearly yourself. Now they begin the quest of trying to save you from yourself. Their entreaties may meet brick walls, though.

You Feel as Though You Can't Do Anything Right

Your self-esteem has been eroded. This is what constant criticism from those you love causes. You're always trying to please him and constantly failing at it. The harder you try, the more unattainable it seems. So, you conclude, you can't do anything right anymore.

They Isolate You

Gaslighters tend to isolate their victims from all who mean well for them, friends and family alike. "They are a bad influence for you," he repeats. The more this happens, the more you fall under their control. With friends and families left out in the cold, there's really no one watching out for you anymore.

It Is a One-sided Loyalty

You can't count the number of times you've put your interest and maybe life down on the line for him. And what has he done for you? Nothing. Gaslighters expect fierce loyalty from their victims but are not ready to give one. Don't attempt to betray them. They would make you wish you hadn't. For them, it is loyalty or nothing. That, in itself, is not bad. Only that it is one-sided.

The list is endless and inexhaustible. Further research will provide you with more signs to watch out for. The core fact to bring out from your gaslighting abuse is that your sense of reality has been severely distorted. If you feel these signs read true, and your partner is gaslighting you, undermining your memories, perceptions, and realities happening around you, then there's every chance you're a victim and should seek help.

Chapter 8.
How to Avoid Mental Manipulation and the Narcissist's Favorite Tool for Manipulation

In today's world, there are manipulators everywhere around you. Most of the people around you are looking for evil ways to take advantage of you for their own twisted pleasures. You need to be very conscious all the time if you want to protect yourself from manipulators. In this article, I am going to talk about several ways by following which you will be able to protect yourself from all the manipulators out there in your everyday life.

Stop Falling into Their Traps

Interrogating you, blaming you, and confusing you are their tactics of getting under your skin; they will do all sorts of things just to make you fall into their trap. Make sure not to fall for their words. They will pretend to be excellent in front of you and try to make you feel bad or guilty about something you have nothing to do with. You might even end up apologizing to them for something you didn't even do.

Don't let it happen. In case you have to deal with manipulators every day (in your institutions or workplace), make sure to ignore them as much as you can. If you can't ignore them, simply surprise them with a positive attitude and don't keep a combative mood. In this way, they will get confused too as to why their tricks aren't working for you, and they might even stop experimenting with their evil schemes on you in the future.

Start Noting Down Everything They Say While Conversing with You

Emotional manipulators have a habit of twisting and turning words just to make you seem like the bad guy. After doing or saying something terrible, they might act, do, or say things in such a way that you might feel that you misunderstood them and feel guilty for doing so.

Even if it seems like a little too much, still make sure to note down every detail of whatever that person says to you. In this way, you can identify whenever the manipulator changes any piece according to their convenience just to make you look bad. Sometimes, they may completely deny that they said or did a particular thing to make you feel bad or guilty. If you have everything written, you will be able to get clarity on what is right and what is wrong and save yourself from many hassles. This is a smart technique of protecting yourself from unwanted drama.

Try Steering Clear Whenever It is Possible

Imagine having no manipulator in your circle! How amazing would that be! Whenever you meet a person for the first time, try to carefully look at the red flags. If you see anything negative about their vibe or energy, make sure to avoid your interactions with them in the future fully. In this way, you will have absolutely no manipulator in your life, and you will be spared from a lot of unnecessary hassles. In some cases, totally avoiding the manipulator is tough.

This is when the manipulator is from somewhere that you can't ignore entirely, like the workplace, schools, colleges, or even family. In these cases, try to limit your interactions with them as much as possible. Also, make sure that your interactions are strictly based on formal things. For example, if that person asks you something related to work. Either try to ignore it or keep your conversations limited to work-related things only. Don't get too friendly or too close.

This can give him a lot of chances to exploit you emotionally. Don't start talking informally; otherwise, it will cost you later.

Try Keeping a Backup

Manipulative people often get scared of playing their dirty tricks when a lot of people are around them. They mainly do these things when you are kind of alone with them and when their activities are not seen by anyone else. So, if it is impossible for you to shut them out of your life completely, or cut down on your interactions with them, try to be around as many people as you can while dealing with them. When others are around you, the manipulators will think twice before saying or doing something weird. They will be too conscious about what others will think of them.

Therefore, you won't have to deal with it. It is a good way to save yourself from them if you find it hard to fight alone.

Start Calling Them Out on Their Behavior

All manipulators are basically cowards; that is why they get pleasure by hurting others. They love playing mind games and love to see whenever people fall into their traps. One thing that every manipulator hate is confrontation. They don't like being called out or being confronted about their behaviors. So, whenever you see that someone is trying to manipulate you emotionally, directly call them out on their behavior. This will allow you to catch them off-guard.

Take your own stand and say to them now that their words or actions make you feel uncomfortable and don't want to deal with these anymore. They might try to deny that they said or did those things, but you could still have satisfaction knowing that you stood up for yourself and didn't just endure everything like a weak person.

This satisfaction will give you more courage to confront again in the future. If you keep facing them and calling out their names, they might stop doing their evil tricks on you because they will understand that you aren't a weak person who will just go on tolerating everything and get played every time.

Don't Get Emotionally Attached to Them

Emotional manipulators take advantage of those who get emotionally attached to them. They use this as their weapon to do anything they want with you as they know you wouldn't be able to say no to them. I have seen a lot of cases where people keep enduring everything just because they are emotionally attached to that person. Make sure not to do this. This is because when you get too emotionally attached, either you don't see the wrong side in them and ignore all the red flags, or you keep forgiving them and expecting them to change even when you know that isn't going to happen.

A lot of times, the emotional manipulator is someone close to you, like your partner or a friend. This makes it hard for you to ignore them or confront them or even think of leaving them because they matter to you. For avoiding these kinds of situations, try staying conscious from the beginning so that you don't get too emotionally attached to someone who might manipulate you emotionally in the future. When you see that they are steamrolling your emotions completely, see this as a red flag. Back away slowly from the relationship and let them know about your boundaries. In case if it is someone from your workplace or someone from the family, make sure to keep a civil and cordial relationship with them.

Try Meditating Often

Relaxation techniques like meditation often help you to release stress and gain inner peace. When you have inner peace, you see things clearly with a calm mind. No matter how much chaotic your surrounding situations are, you will be able to calmly deal with the manipulators and their tricks. When you meditate and gain inner peace, you might also start seeing their struggles and the reasons behind their behaviors. This might also lead you to see them with the eyes of compassion and pity.

This will help you to forgive them and see the good in them. You might see the bigger picture and kindly deal with them. This will save you from a lot of trouble. Sometimes kindness is all you need to rise above someone. You instantly become the bigger person when you forgive someone and look at them with pity. Also, make sure that you only forgive them and do not forget what they did. Forgetting what they did will put you in the same place again, so don't do that. Forgive and move on with your life.

Try Inspiring Them

Inspiring someone is the best thing that you can do. Manipulators are humans, too, and there might be some reasons behind these kinds of behavior. Try to see the good in them and inspire them. You might encourage them not to waste their time messing around with people and invest their time in bettering themselves, eating healthy, staying fit, chasing their dreams, and doing everything in order to be the best versions of themselves. If they genuinely get inspired by you, they won't be the same person again. After all, everybody makes mistakes, and everyone deserves a second chance. You should give it to them and see if they change. The most important thing you need to keep in mind is that it is not your duty to inspire them or change them. If you see that no matter what you do, they are not changing or taking a toll on your mental health to inspire them or make them a better person, you don't need to do it. Nothing is more important than your well-being.

Try Not to Get Too Empathetic

Empathy is good, but too much of it can bring you trouble. As I have mentioned earlier, you need to be a better person and inspire them; you also need to keep in mind that it is not your duty to do so. Don't waste your time if you see that the person isn't putting any effort into bringing the change. Some people just never change, and it might be a little hard to accept, but it is a fact, and you should accept it. Just move on already!

Start Telling Them That They Are Right

Telling someone that they are right even when you know they don't need a lot of courage. Your ego will crash to do so, but if you can do it, you will satisfy your soul. Emotional manipulators crave drama. They want you to get back at them with a combative attitude so that they can again twist your words and play them against you to make you feel worse. Once you say "yes, you are right," they will have nothing more to say.

This will catch them off-guard, and they will be confused for a while about what to say or do next in order to continue this. Sometimes saying someone they are right makes you a bigger person, and this pisses off the other party. Letting them win the argument will not only maintain your inner peace but will also show them that you aren't someone who will waste your energy, effort, or time just to win a stupid little argument with them. Surprise them with this positive attitude, and they will understand that you aren't easy to mess with, and they will make sure to keep their distance from you in the future.

Try Letting Go of the Harmful Relationships

If you start noticing these kinds of behaviors in your spouse, girlfriend, or boyfriend, leave them then and there. Don't stay for the sake of love because love has no room for manipulation. Nobody is worth more than your own happiness and well-being. A person can't be changed forcefully if they are not willing to. Try talking to them about it once and see if they are making efforts to change. If yes, very well, but if not, just leave right away! You deserve someone who will love you, care for you, cherish you, and help you be a better person, not someone who will take advantage of you or will make you feel miserable about yourself. If your partner does this, you must know that he/she is not in love with you. They are just with you because you seem to be easy prey to them. So, make sure not to be in any kind of relationship with a manipulator. If you start explaining to them why you are leaving, they might turn that against you as well. This will again damage your mental peace and make things worse for you. Always remember that you don't need to explain anything to a person who doesn't care about you. Leave silently, and they will know exactly why you did what you did.

Develop a Strong Mentality

Never let a manipulator get inside your skin, don't let their words into your heart, and don't let their dirty tricks get inside your head. Remembering these three things can be a life-changer for you. Manipulators get inside your head for making you do or feel what they want you to do or feel. If they can't get inside your head, they might as well stop bothering you. Know that you are valuable and that your emotions and feelings are not something to play with. While dealing with a manipulator, keep your head straight and don't let their tricks get the better of you. Ignore whatever they are saying or trying to do. Know your self-worth and keep your mind strong. Once you are able to do that, nothing can bring you down.

Practice Positive Self-Talk

Sometimes all you need is a little affirmation from yourself. People are often too harsh on themselves and forget to remind themselves about how good they actually are. Always remember that you deserve the same amount of kindness that you give to others. Don't blame yourself for everything, and don't just keep feeling guilty for every single thing. You are worth a lot more, and you should know it. Practicing positive self-talk is a great way of boosting your self-worth. Make sure to say positive things about yourself in your mind every single day. You will understand how good of a person you are. Once you know your self-worth, you won't be bothered by these cheap tricks of the manipulators around you. Give yourself positive and uplifting affirmations every day like "I am amazing," "I deserve all the good things," "I am much more than what they think of me," "What they say about me isn't going to bother me because I know who I am." These affirmations will make sure to make you realize your own value and give you the courage to throw those people away who don't give you the respect and love you deserve.

Manipulators are everywhere around you. You need to keep your eyes open to see the red flags. Don't make the mistake of ignoring the signs. Don't get intimidated by them and give in to their manipulation. Work on your self-confidence, be strong, and know your self-worth. This will give you the courage to stand up against them and fight for yourself. You are the most valuable thing in your life, and nobody or nothing is more important than yourself. Follow the above-mentioned steps and protect yourself from manipulators.

Chapter 9.
Why We Fall, Victim?

You must have wondered endlessly how you could ever be a target for the narcissist. You're a good person who does not deserve to be treated so terribly, after all. What is it about you that attracts the narcissist? What is it about you that makes them say, "Aha, there's a good target to lay all this evil on"? It is no fault of yours being chosen as the narcissist's target.

They just happen to be the most efficient and deadliest of emotional predators.

They know the best people to target, and you're not a random choice. They're not targeting you because you're a terrible person, so don't assume you're broken.

Things about You That Make You a Target

You're a caring, loving person who is passionate about helping people

At the beginning of your relationship, everything seems nice and beautiful. However, that changes quickly. At the beginning of your relationship, if you're a giver, you'll naturally want to give more and more to your significant other. The origin of love is that it works great for the narcissist, as they get to be your one and only. All your attention is on them all the time, and they love it, being the emotional vampire that they are. As time goes by, the narcissist sucks you dry, insidiously gaining power over you without you being aware of what's going on.

You've got something the gaslighter wants

It can be your lifestyle. It can be money, position, or power. Whatever it is, they want something from you. Your relationship probably began with the narcissist being ever so helpful. However, the second thing doesn't work out for them; they take away the carrot and get the stick. The second it becomes obvious to them that you now know what they're really after, and it's not you; they'll just escalate the tension that's already there.

The narcissist wants only one thing from your relationship: complete control of whatever they perceive you have.

You had a dysfunctional childhood

Suppose you had the misfortune of growing up in a dysfunctional family. In that case, it can make it hard for you to notice when you're being abused or when your boundaries are being disrespected since that's all you've ever really known anyway. You probably also have trouble setting boundaries, and when you do put them, you're probably not firm about them. For this reason, the narcissist is drawn to you. They're not a fan of boundaries. Therefore, they choose you so that they can exploit this weakness of yours for their own selfish purposes. As part of their abuse, they will swoop in and do everything for you. It seems like they're beneficial on the surface, but what's really going on is that they are creating a situation where you can't do anything for yourself. You come to depend on them for everything. Their helpful heroics only serve to take away all sense of empowerment and independence from you.

You have compassion and empathy in spades

Nothing is ever the narcissist's fault. There's always something or someone else responsible for their misfortune in life, as far as they are concerned. As you listen to their sad tales, you find yourself drawn in, wanting to help them in some way since you are compassionate and empathetic. This works for the narcissist because they become the center of attention in your world. Inevitably, what starts off as a good intention on your part becomes an unhealthy, life-sucking relationship in the end.

You keep accepting blame for stuff, even when it was

clearly not your fault

In your steadily worsening relationship with the narcissist, you will find that they're always covertly or overtly saying that you're the problem. They'll shift the blame onto you and pile on the guilt as well. They will say, "Well, if you hadn't acted the way you did, then I wouldn't have gotten upset." So rather than having the focus be on the horrible thing that they did to you, they've shifted the blame onto your shoulders by saying it was your fault they acted that way in the first place. They'll dig their heels in, too, so that you cannot get back to the topic at hand.

You're lonely and desperate for love

The narcissist always seeks out people who have a deep need that needs to be taken care of. They love knowing that you need friends, or you need to be loved, and will more than happily fill that role. In the beginning, you might assume that their intensity is a good thing. You might think it is a pure passion! However, that's not the case. Over time, the intensity tapers off and does so drastically. The warm and loving narcissist is suddenly icier than the arctic, detached as a stranger. This leaves you confused, wondering what you did wrong and how you can fix it, just so you can get back the person who once held the brightest, hottest torch for you.

You run the other way when it comes to conflict

If you make a habit of avoiding confrontation just to keep the peace, then this makes you a prime candidate for the narcissist to target. Often, people who are not confrontational have an intense fear of guilt, abandonment, and the end of relationships that matter to them. When the narcissist rages out, you feel this fear in you become active, almost crippling your ability to think straight. You will do whatever you need to in order to keep the peace; the more you run from confrontation, the more the narcissist is drawn to you.

How the Narcissist Tests You

Each time you allow the narcissist to get their way in the beginning, you don't realize that you're being tested. This is one test you absolutely want to flunk! The way to bomb is to stand your ground, assert your rights, and not be so agreeable or flexible.

It is one thing to know that—at some point—the narcissist has tested you or will test you. However, that doesn't help much if you can't even recognize when you're being tested. Let's look at some of the "tests" set for us, so we can fail and fail excellently every time!

The narcissist tells you that they'll call you by a set date and time, but then they don't

This is not random. It's a test. What happens after that missed appointment is that they will eventually get in touch with you and act like everything is fine and dandy when it isn't; you've been waiting for your phone to go off when they said they'd call, but it never did. Now they're talking to you as if there's nothing wrong at all as if they never promised to call when they asked you to. You're left feeling like an anxious mess! What's the goal? They want to see how you take it. They want to know how you react. They will have some very convenient excuse, saying something popped up or they forgot, but that's no error. They deliberately chose not to call because they needed to read your reaction. If you call them out on it, they will accuse you of acting out too vigorously. Note: this is not to say that you're dealing with a narcissist every time this happens. If you call someone out on that, they will genuinely apologize if they didn't mean to do it. However, if you're talking to a narcissist, they'll be upset that you're making this a big deal. That said, if you know someone who keeps doing this, then you should cut them loose; they aren't worth your time or effort.

The narcissist asks you to change something about yourself or the way you look

Say you just met, or you just got into the relationship, and then your significant other tells you to change something about the way you like to dress or the way you do something. That can be a possible red flag! No one in their right mind would tell someone they just met or only just started dating to change this or that about themselves. Whatever you do, be yourself. Don't assume, "Well, this relationship will be for the long haul, so let me change what they want." Don't do it! Be yourself, and if they're not a narcissist, they'll be completely okay with you as you are.

The narcissist overshares about their terrible exes and terrible childhood

This is also a test to see how you choose to respond to their tales of woe. As they share, you'll notice them also probing you with questions about your own childhood as well. Now, there's a chance the narcissist really was abused or had it rough growing up. Of course, that's a terrible thing, no matter who it happened to. With that said, be on your toes because they might be looking for your weak spots as they try to create some *cognitive empathic connection* with you. They just want to know what makes you go soft and fragile; eventually, they can use that to their advantage. The first time you meet someone is not the best time to talk about your dark and terrible past or the trauma you've gone through. That's not a healthy start to a relationship or friendship.

The narcissist says, "You can trust me," when you've both only just met

People who cannot be trusted are likely to use the phrase "You can trust me" when you just met each other. They would not even be deliberating such sensitive issues that require trust when you're just meeting unless you're in group therapy or something. There is a natural sequence of events when it comes to relationships and friendships. The last thing you want to do is accept that statement at face value and open up because you just might be dealing with a narcissist. If you open up, they will assume it's easy for them to get into your head, and they will have a lot they can use against you.

Sometimes There's No Reason

There are times when you become the target of a narcissist, not because of anything in particular, but simply because you happened to be in the wrong place at the wrong time. Don't assume there's something wrong with you because they chose to target you! There's a little something called transference, which narcissists are guilty of. It's when they take their rage or anger and direct it at the closest, most convenient, most reachable person that they can bully… and sometimes, you're it!

Whatever the case may be, know that you are your own person. You don't have to be a victim. I was in my 30s before that I realized I didn't have to keep taking abuse from others. Coming from a dysfunctional home, I had no idea what boundaries were and what was not okay. However, I learned over time, and since then, my life has been free and clear of narcissists. When I do encounter one, I find that I value my freedom and joy too much to let them make my life horrible. I would love for you to see this same freedom and happiness, too. If things have already gone too far that you don't even think you can set yourself free, then please see a professional therapist to help you to find yourself again.

Chapter 10.

THE ROAD TO RECOVERY

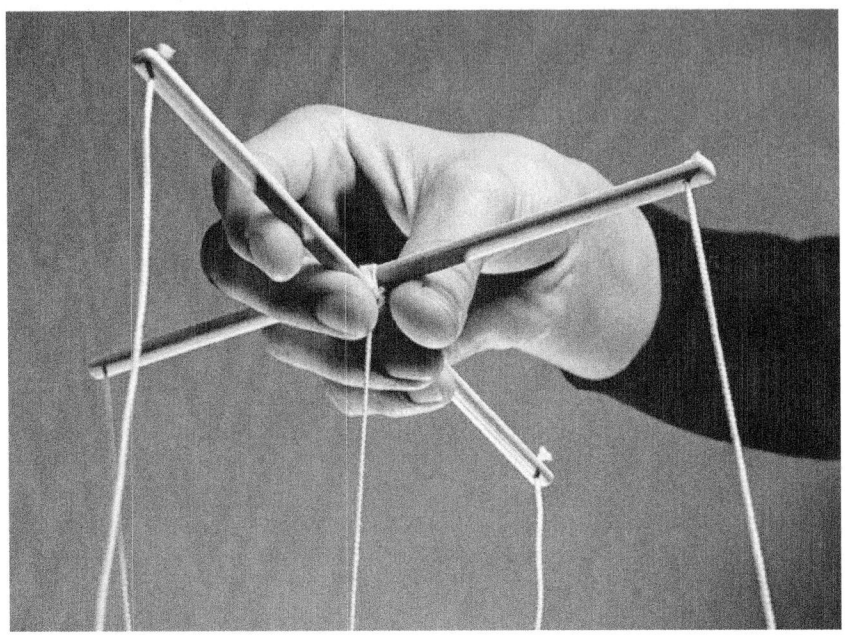

You have now identified that you are a victim of gaslighting. You have also learned that the critical first step to healing from gaslighting is to cut yourself off from your abuser. After all, your abuser has methodically brainwashed you into questioning your own reality. Clearly, they have immense power over you, and whether you like it or not, you rely on them in many ways. This means that the idea of leaving them can induce massive amounts of anxiety. First, know that this is normal. Second, know that you can channel the energy of your stress into something positive. This is all about using your power to reassert control over your life. This all starts with creating the necessary distance between you and your abuser. After that, it is essential to establish the boundaries that will keep you out of their power for good. Boundaries are important regardless, so use these tools continuously as you reclaim your life and liberty.

Cutting Ties and Moving On

You are ready to admit you have suffered gaslighting, and you are prepared to make your life whole again. You can be complete without your abuser. You can survive without your abuser. Here is how you start.

Suppose you are overwhelmed by the idea of leaving your abuser with immediate effect. In that case, there are a few steps you can take before you leave to make the transition easier and to help facilitate an emotional break from your abuser.

1. You need to analyze your abuser in a new way. Step outside of your relationship for a while, and ask yourself if they are the kind of person you want to be around. Remove all the toxic history, remove all the memories, and instead ponder if they are a fun person, a good person, a nice person. If you cannot do this as a stranger, then imagine someone you love being in a relationship with your abuser. If they are truly gaslighting you, you will likely be appalled at the idea of them manipulating and abusing someone you love. Then return to your reality. If you do not want that kind of relationship with someone you love, why would you accept

it for yourself? You deserve more. You should want more for yourself and not be ashamed of it. If you can admit that they are a fundamentally flawed person who has victimized you again and again, then you can acknowledge that it is time to move on to something better. There is no shame in wanting more out of your life, and removing such a massive obstacle is the surest way to emotional freedom and happiness.

2. After you have found a way to see the monstrous nature of your abuser, you may find yourself plagued by doubt and indecision. This is completely natural, but it is also something you have to conquer. In order to see the way out, you have to know why you have stayed in the first place. Yes, your abuser has made you a victim, but they must have also done things that compelled you to stay. Take a moment and write down all of the things they have done that make you want to keep them in your life. This could include things like taking care of finances, providing support, flattering and complimenting you, etc. There is an endless number of things they will have used to make you feel good enough that it is hard to leave. Now, rather than just try to give up all these benefits immediately, make a plan for how you will find those benefits in other places.

If there are financial benefits, then how can you make yourself financially independent? Is there someone else in your life who can provide a loan until you find that independence? Suppose the financial benefits are massive, and you would be essentially broke and homeless without your abuser. In that case, you will have to find a group or center or family who is willing to help you find that independence, even if it takes time. It will not be easy to let go, but it will help you to know you have a plan rather than taking a blind leap.

If there are emotional supports you will miss, think back to the support system you had before isolating you. Other people have been there for you before, and there may be new people in your life you can reach out to. Your abuser has made you feel like they are the only person who can ever make you happy, but there are most likely plenty of people all around you willing to actively listen and help you through these struggles.

If there are other benefits, like words of affirmation or the fact that your abuser makes you feel wanted and/or desirable, then you will have to look to another source: yourself. This may seem counterintuitive or even naïve, but the fact is you have not loved yourself enough to exit this toxic relationship. If you do not learn how to love yourself at some point, you will most likely return to the cycle. So, do not seek your approval only from outside. Approve yourself. Write down what you like about yourself, compliment yourself, take pride in yourself. Look in the mirror, right into your own eyes, and tell yourself, "I love you." Keep doing this until you actually believe it.

3. Your feelings are very much tied up in your abuser. That is how gaslighting works. You have been manipulated into a place where you trust no one but them, not even yourself. However, another way to see the abuse and work to get out is to make yourself reflect on the feelings they induce. After every encounter you have with them, stop, reflect, and record. Have you left them feeling good, bad, numb? Are you feeling guilty, unsure, lost? Did they say anything at all that created positive thoughts about yourself or built up your happiness and self-esteem? If you are being gaslighted, what you will notice is that a pattern emerges. There will be some high points, of course, but the majority of what you are feeling will be negative and draining. This gives you irrefutable data that connects your unhappiness and uncertainty directly to your abuser. It is hard to ignore and continue to accept that the person who is supposed to love and/or support you is beating you down instead.

4. You may struggle to find people who will replace the positive things your abuser provided, but that does not mean you have to give up. Other people are not the only answer. Your abuser has most likely taken you away from the things you used to enjoy. Now, as you seek to extricate yourself from the abuse, it is time to rediscover those old joys. Maybe you used to write, draw, dance, sing, or play a sport. Without involving your abuser, take steps to do those things again. Those simple activities are a great way to show

yourself there is a way to be happy without the other person in your life. They will also show you that it is possible to be self-reliant. Your happiness should not hinge entirely on one person. You must be able to recognize that you can be happy on your own.

5. One of the best ways to undo the charms of a bad relationship is to start building a good one. This may take some time and consideration, but seek out someone you think would be a good friend. Look for a person who has made you laugh and smile or who seems to have a lot in common with you. Now you can seek to amplify those positive effects by spending more time with that person. Ask them to get coffee or see a movie or do an activity you know you both enjoy. Building that strong foundation will make it easier to open up to them about your life and needs. What you will find is a totally different experience than that which you were experiencing with your abuser. You will have a point of comparison that empowers you to say this new relationship is much better than your abusive one. It will also help you see the fatal flaws in your abuser's so-called support and love.

6. One of the strategies you use to be successful on a new diet is the same as a strategy you need to successfully leave a toxic relationship. That strategy is to let yourself indulge in something once in a while, so you do not feel completely deprived. Of course, you should not necessarily indulge in

food, but that may be what works for you. If you are successfully staying away from your abuser, take yourself out on a date. Go to one of your favorite places. Ask a friend to do a fun activity with you. Stay in and have a sort of spa day. You were always punishing yourself when you were with your abuser. It is time to reward yourself as you successfully stay away from them. A good idea would be to make this harder over time. For example, you may start by rewarding yourself for not talking to them for one whole day. That sounds like nothing, but it can be harder than you may think. After you make it through the day, do something you enjoy. As it gets easier to avoid them for a whole day, make it three days before you get your next reward. If you keep building up your stamina this way, before long, you will be going weeks, months, and even years without contacting your abuser or letting them disrupt your thoughts all the time.

7. A final tip is to let yourself take a break and checkout after you have broken ties with your abuser. The emotional exhaustion you feel will most likely manifest itself in physical ways, so take a day off to sleep, nap, lounge. Rest brings healing and time for reflection. That is what you need to get out and stay out of your abusive relationship.

Building Boundaries

All of the steps listed above will fail if you do not know how to follow through with boundaries. Boundaries are what will keep you from falling into old patterns that let the abuse continue.

One way to set a firm boundary is to make it something you can measure. That does not mean you have to create a graph of your relationship or anything like that. What you can do is use what you have learned from analyzing your abuse to pick some of the worst and most consistent abuses you have experienced. Imagine that it is put-downs, like telling you about how undesirable you are to other people since you let yourself go, but your abuser stays with you anyway. After each conversation you have with your abuser, write down as much as you can remember about what was said. Then go back and find how often they put you down in the conversation. Analyze how it made you feel. Now that you understand your own feelings better, the next time you have a conversation, they put you down and respond by clearly and concisely communicating your feelings. If they refuse to listen or put down how you feel, then they have violated your boundaries. Remove yourself from the situation immediately, so the abuser is no longer rewarded for violating your sense of safety. Then go back and write down what happened in this encounter. Before long, you will have a log of the many times they have violated your boundaries without remorse. That means they do not respect you or love you enough to listen when you set the border in the first place.

Some boundaries are more concrete than emotional boundaries. If you are feeling overwhelmed or smothered by your relationship, then physical distance and limited or no contact may be the best solution.

To create physical boundaries, you may need to do something as simple as asking the other person to step back while you communicate with them. It could also be as drastic as removing yourself from their presence entirely. To decide on what kind of boundary is best for you, you may want to start with a small physical limitation and see the effect it creates. If your abuser reacts in a big way, then you are likely in such a toxic relationship that you need to remove yourself from their presence entirely. If your abuser struggles with the boundary but tries to respect it in some small way, you can make your removal from them more gradual. This could be easier for you, or it could make leaving harder. The best tactic is to constantly tune back into your own emotions and evaluate what will help you get to freedom and happiness faster and also safely.

To create limited contact, it is best to combine the first tip with this tip. Make the boundary measurable, like allowing one phone call a day or texting only between nine and eleven hours. As was stated above, you will have to gauge what you can handle emotionally and gauge the reaction of your abuser. Slow the process of limiting contact if you think you are unable to go with no contact, speed up the process of limited communication, go straight to no contact if you are ready, or feel unsafe.

Boundaries benefit most from not just being measurable but also by being consistently enforced. You need to hold yourself accountable in some way. This could be by creating a journal or chart to track your progress. It could also be by electing an accountability partner who will consistently check in on your progress and provide feedback if you start to flounder. Consistency is the key to your freedom, and consistency will help you establish boundaries when you are ready to build a new and healthy relationship.

Chapter 11.
5 POWERFUL SELF-CARE TIPS FOR ABUSE AND TRAUMA SURVIVORS

Often, we undermine our self-esteem without realizing it. People are all different: some are emotionally stronger, others are not.

Now you will discover the 5 stones, 5 habits to be taken to avoid destroying your self-esteem.

You have to understand that this is something fundamental if you want to live a full and happy life.

Respect Yourself

If you are not able to respect yourself, how can you ever respect others? It is absolutely impossible. A gesture that may seem trivial to you is, in reality, the key to avoiding destroying your self-esteem.
How can we learn to respect ourselves?

First of all, we need to understand what our needs and values are and then satisfy them. We should not continuously put ourselves in the background and please others first. If we do not realize that we do not know how to satisfy ourselves, we must change our attitude. Express your feelings and do not feel guilty because of them. Showing anger towards someone does not turn you into bad people but into sincere people. Give value to all those aspects of you that you are proud of. Think about it and convince yourself that you deserve it.

Acceptance

Accepting yourself is very important if you want to make the most of your life. Otherwise, you will live a mere copy of the lives of others.
Do you really want to live a lie?

Your life must be original; it must be yours for real. Do not try to be the same as others or have a life like them. Perhaps other life seems perfect, but is it really so? Learn to love your life and accept yourself: only in this way can you live fortunately and in agreement.

Distinguish Your Mistakes

If you do not identify your mistakes, you will be living your entire life accumulating excuses and fake daily situations, wasting an enormous amount of energy.

The best advice I can give you is to learn from your mistakes. Face the error and the excuse and accept them. Where did you go wrong? What happened? Do not dodge mistakes with excuses but take advantage to learn from them and improve as people. Mistakes make us neither weak nor vulnerable. They strengthen us and prepare us for future mistakes.

Pay Attention with Your Critical Voice

Being critical about ourselves is not bad, but we must be careful: sometimes, this critical voice living in us can destroy our souls. We must be the ones to destroy her. When our critical voice is excessively negative and discouraging and blocks us, we must rest because it is not bringing anything good.

Do you know how self-esteem is destroyed by the inner critical voice?

1. "You'll never succeed." A phrase whispered slowly by your critical voice. When you listen to it, try to think, "And what do I know if I will never succeed? Have I ever tried it? Have I failed? If you really want something, try to do it and silence your inner voice through action.

2. "You're worse than others." Nobody is better or worse than someone else; we are just different people. It is very nice to see how it is possible to complete or help in the work that

is being carried out. Never make a comparison between yourself and others; learn, strive, and be yourself. Please now stand up and say: "I am unique and original, different from anyone else." Repeat again and again.

3. "This person doesn't like you." Are you sure? Did you ask him? Perhaps you are misrepresenting the signals. Besides, if you really don't like it, what does it matter? It is certainly not the end of the world. Everything can be overcome; there is no need to make a drama.

Please, Do Not Seek the Approval of Others

Continually seeking the approval of others is a very common mistake; it is simply a signal of great insecurity. Important decisions are better if they are different from those of others. Don't try to make others happy; if you have a contrary opinion, show it! Remember that if others do not approve of you, you only allow them to do so.

Be convinced in your decisions, actions, and reflections. The others will never be able to agree with you on everything; that's why you have to be yourself. Perhaps you can find yourself in the description just given. Yes, it's normal; it's something inevitable. To get the approval of others, to think of not being at their height, to build an excuse behind the other, not to say what you think.

We are the result of a complex equation involving several variables. Our thoughts and the people we surround ourselves with are among those that have more weight on our state of mind and on our person.

We are what we think, but only the people we put next to our lives can define us honestly. No context is neutral, and few situations are foreign to the influence others can have on us, based on what they say, do or give up on doing. So, even if we would like the influence to be completely positive and a source of inspiration, the truth is that sometimes we try the opposite.

Many people will tell you to always try to surround yourself with people who enrich you, those who bring out only the best of us. And yet, let's face it, it is not at all times possible for very specific reasons.

We are what we think, and we are the product of our social relationships. All of us, in part, are the result of those who gave us life and were educated; we are the product of our interactions with the people we met at school, university, workplace, or in other social contexts.

It is not at all times possible for us to choose these figures; in the majority of cases, we are given and, consequently, from time to time, we are obligated to live with those we don't like at all.

In this sense, and although in the end, the experience has taught us how to relate to those who do not put us at ease or those who provoke anxiety in us rather than happiness, even the result of these interactions and experiences determines who we are. So, who we are today is the complex but beautiful set of links with each person who has been part of our existential path?

We often don't realize the voice of our thoughts, our attitudes, our attributions, and our reasonings. It is these that outline the architecture of who we are, that limit us or empower us, are the ones that ultimately influence the way we feel and how we behave.

The art of believing in yourself is, above all, an exercise in the will. And the intention is a muscle of power that is exercised through appropriate thoughts, centered and aimed at a specific goal: to promote one's own wellbeing and personal growth.

However, and we know this well, it is not easy to direct the compass of our thoughts towards positivism and trust when what dwells in us is low self-esteem. When we experience apathy, frustration, and demotivation.

As it may seem, our parents and even educational systems forget to teach us to believe in ourselves. Instead, they guide us to be like the majority. Because "being normal" is acting, thinking, and behaving like others, diluting our particularities in the ordinary, in the everyday. Because sometimes being unique means being different, and the difference doesn't fit well, out of tune. It is disharmony in a world that loves the foreseeable.

Now I want to ask you to think of the five people you frequent most in your life: in fact, each of us is the result of the sum of the 5 people with whom he spends the most time. There is a subtle but evident nuance, and it is that these figures with whom we share the most significant number of hours of the day are our partner, our family, and our friends.

Sometimes, and because of our working days, we spend more time away from home. This makes it possible, for example, that the influence of work colleagues, bosses, and other company figures broadly define our state of mind. Furthermore, there is another detail that has a great impact on our wellbeing. Dividing our time between multiple social contexts is not always reflected in our wellbeing. Sometimes, our days are a complex succession of movements for which we move from home to work, from the gym to various courses, from the supermarket to family visits, to the time shared with people who like us or not. All this often leads us to accumulate a strong stress load that we are not always aware of. The people we admit in our lives are the ones that can influence our mood.

They define us the duties, the advice given or not given, the words, the silences, what we see, and the expectations that arise. Alternatively, this can also happen at the couple level, where we end up assuming, almost deprived of realizing it, any other person's features and vice versa.

Seneca said that life is a theatrical work and that for this, it does not matter how long it lasts, but rather the way in which it was staged. To this wise message, another one is added: in this context, we are not always alone. There are more actors in the representation of life, and it depends on us whether to act as protagonists or as mere extras.

The people around us determine who we are, we know. It is not possible to choose one's own family, but one can decide, at the right moment, with whom to maintain contact and with whom not. We can't even "turn off" as if it were a video game those uncomfortable coworkers, classmates, neighbors, or acquaintances who we often don't like.

Although these people cannot be avoided, we can do, however, learn to manage them, establish boundaries, open up emotional umbrellas, and prevent their attitudes from exerting a certain power over us. On the other hand, and here comes the most important point, each of us has a margin of freedom to decide who to let in and who let out of their lives.

Surrounding yourself with good people is not an art; it is a need. It is not a gift, but a privilege, to have figures at your side that are inspirational, that allow us to bring out the best in us. We are made of what we think. Let's keep this in mind every day.

Chapter 12.
HEALING FROM EMOTIONAL TRAUMA AND REBUILDING YOUR LIFE

Breaking free from a gaslighter may be one of the most challenging things you have to do because they have their way of convincing you that you need them to survive. If your mind has accepted this lie, then it becomes truly difficult to survive without them.

There is still the issue of getting your sanity and self-image back after a gaslighter has bastardized it.

You may have a lot on your plate when you break free from a gaslighter, but I will share with you some tips that you can use to recover from gaslighting and regain your usual self.

Seek Professional Help

Depending on the severity of the gaslighting and how long it's been going on, talking to a therapist or a psychiatrist can be a good way of getting back on track. Seek professionals who specialize in psychological abuse victims to get the best treatment.

A therapist will help you get through your emotions. After being gaslighted, you probably have a lot of feelings that you are unsure of and have kept bottled up. So long as these emotions remain bottled up in your mind without you realizing it, you can never be that person you used to be.

A psychiatrist can help you find medication to ease the symptoms of abuse, such as anxiety, insomnia, and depression before you are ready to stand up on your own.

Permit Yourself to Feel

Your feelings were not treated as valid since your gaslighter constantly belittled your feelings and emotions. It doesn't have to be like that anymore. Now that you have broken away from the gaslighter, it is time to learn how to feel again and take your feelings seriously. You don't have to be afraid of feeling anymore.

While allowing your feelings to flow freely, don't be restrictive. Allow yourself to vent out all the emotions you have bottled up in the past. Don't try to avoid extreme feelings, such as anger, fear, or sadness. It may take a while to get them uncovered, but you must let them pass instead of hiding them. One way to vent off your emotions is to join a support group.

In these groups, you can meet other victims of gaslighting and/or different traumatizing experiences. When you hear people talk about their experiences, and you finally start to let yours out, you will surely feel better and realize that you're not alone.

Never Go for Revenge

Sometimes you might be tempted to seek revenge or treat the abuser the way they treated you. I hear people saying you can beat them at their own game. Some people have even come up with steps one can adopt to take revenge on a gaslighter. This is a bad idea, and it is never an option because:

- You will be inviting them back into your life. Now that you have successfully broken free from a gaslighter, the last thing you want to do is to have them back in your life. Don't forget how manipulative they can be. They can gradually work their way back into your life if you're not careful.

- You might be thinking that your guards are intact, and there is no breaking through, but what if I told you that countless victims of gaslighting that I have treated had told stories of how they unknowingly let the gaslighters back into their lives. When it comes to gaslighters, the best way is to disconnect from them completely if you are sure that the gaslighter is unwilling to change, which is very likely. Don't leave anything to chance.

- You will reignite the negative emotions you feel. Remember that your number one goal now is to eliminate the negative emotions, not to reignite them. You may think that getting revenge will make you feel better, but it won't. Rather, it will bring up negative emotions all over again.

- You will give them the option to "prove" that you are crazy. Your gaslighter spent all the time trying to convince you that you overreact and that you are crazy. You knew in your heart that this was not the case. But what do you think it will look like if, after breaking free from the gaslighter, you started doing things like trailing a gaslighter and looking for ways to get your pound of flesh? That certainly seems to overact to me.

- If, in the process of trying to seek revenge, the gaslighter tells you, "You, see? I told you that you were crazy," it will hit you differently this time. You might start believing what the gaslighter is saying, and that's returning to the circle of doom. The best thing would be to let the gaslighter be and focus on your recovery instead.

Seek Self-Affirmation

Since you've been belittled and your emotions and feelings were downplayed for a long time, take the time to use self-affirmations. It will, in time, help you get back your self-esteem and confidence. Exercise: start by standing in front of a mirror each day or taking a piece of paper if that's more comfortable. Say/write phrases such as "I am loved," "I can be loved," "I am worthy," "I matter." You will probably have to fake it at first, but eventually, you will realize you're telling the truth. This self-affirmation aims to revalidate yourself. It is the most relevant step in your recovery from gaslighting. When you were being gaslighted, it is possible that you came to mistrust everything you heard, felt, and remembered. You started accepting that you might be crazy. Now that you have taken that you are fine, it is time to start trusting your instinct and your senses again.

Shift Your Perspective

Acknowledge that you are a victim of abuse but that you survived it, and you are moving on. Think of yourself in positive ways—as a warrior, a winner, or something else with a positive meaning. What you went through did not break you, and you should be proud of that.

Develop New Relations

You may have issues with trust at first, but you must remember that not everyone is a gaslighter. Try to build new friendships, even new relationships. Take your time and be careful, but not overly so; there are people out there who are willing to help and support you. With that in mind, don't force yourself into anything. Start this process only when you feel ready.

Alternatively, you can start rebuilding the relationships you lost while you were being gaslighted. Recall that the abuser will try to make you turn against everyone that may stand in their way. Your gaslighter will use statements like, "So you've listened to that crazy talk that is not good for you, right? They will mislead you soon." Now that you are out of that nasty web, it is time to rebuild all the beautiful relationships you lost during the gaslighting. Reaching out to past friends or family (assuming they weren't the abusers and it won't make it easier for the abuser to get to you) can help you recover and rebuild your life.

Take Your Time

You need to give yourself time. Do not expect to go from a traumatized patient to your former self in a short time. Be patient with yourself and trust your recovery process. Time is the best healing factor when combined with proper professional and self-care.

Emotional abuse is a complex matter. Don't expect to be fully healed within weeks, as it may take years. Do it at your own pace, as long as you're moving forward. Don't try to immediately get back to how things used to be. You must acknowledge that things have changed, and you must develop new ways to deal with them.

Don't get frustrated if things aren't moving as fast as you wish they would.

Use Meditation to Enhance Empathy

It is typical for gaslighting victims to develop distrust and lack of empathy when they get out of a gaslighting situation. This is because they no longer know who to trust, and, in some cases, they can make them cold. If you have been gaslighted and you now lack empathy towards people around you, it is time to use mindfulness and meditation techniques to prep up your empathy on your back to recovery. I need not tell you that a lack of empathy can ruin the few relationships you might have left. It can also make you act like the very gaslighter you dislike so much, thereby bringing you down to their level.

How then can mindfulness and meditation do this? Let's start our discourse by looking at mindfulness and meditation. Mindfulness is a psychological process that can help you to be conscious of your past and present experiences without judging yourself. Meditation helps you to willfully bring your mind down to the things that matter most to you.

So how can this help you regain your empathy? It works by making you aware that the distrust and cold feelings you have about people in your life is stemming from the gaslighting you suffered. Since mindfulness helps you have a clear picture of everything that is happening in your life, you become aware that your feelings are a result of your gaslighting. Once you have identified the reason why you are the way you are, half of your problem is solved.

The next phase is to use mindfulness and meditation techniques to monitor and track your feelings to not accommodate hate and hard surfaces. Since you are meditating and monitoring your emotions, you can easily spot those negative emotions and flush them out. To flush them out, you just need to replace them with warm feelings, the kind that is free of negative emotions.

However, redirecting your thoughts will not come easily. It is a skill you will develop gradually using meditation. Meditation helps you to master the all-important skill of shifting your thoughts quickly. The main aim is to remove ideas that conflict with the feelings you desire. When you successfully flush those ill thoughts, you will achieve inner peace. This inner peace will also show in your relationship with others. When you achieve peace with yourself, you can easily achieve peace with the people around you. Because, now, you are not on edge, and you will not misjudge and misunderstand people's intentions.

Generally, meditation and mindfulness can help you improve your mental health. And trust me, if you have suffered gaslighting, no matter how small, you need to regain your mental health by all means. So, if you wish to become that sweet and thoughtful person you were before you encountered a gaslighter, mindfulness and meditation are your best bet for regaining your mild touch and sweetness.

While there are several forms of meditation, one is more effective for this purpose, and it is known as loving-kindness or compassion meditation. This meditation makes your brain release impulses that breed positive emotions, such as empathy and kindness.

CONCLUSION

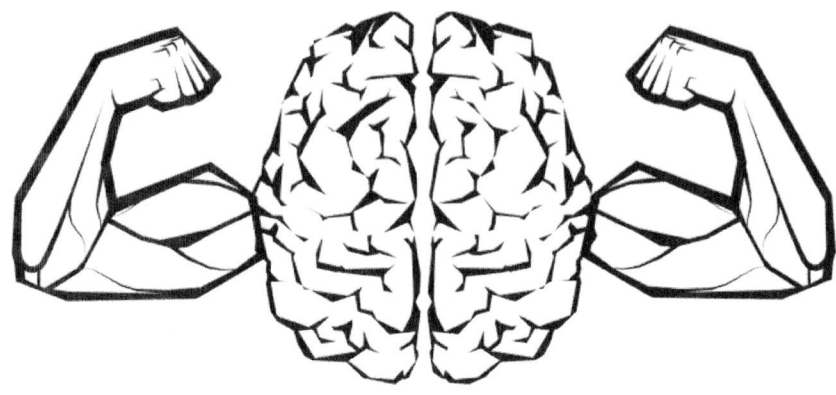

If you are a victim of gaslighting or suspect that someone might be gaslighting you, then reading this book is an excellent first step toward protecting yourself from the effects of gaslighting and recovery.

But reading alone is not enough. Practicing what you read can be the difference between staying stuck in the shadow of a gaslighter and being the independent individual that you are meant to be.

It is not only children in the formative ages who can be influenced by their environment. Even as adults, the people we spend time with can affect us positively or negatively. Living, working, and associating with someone who constantly reminds you of how incompetent, weak, and unfit you are is not healthy for your emotional health. Surrounding yourself with positivity is not merely a New Age gibberish. The implication of doing the opposite can be pretty devastating. Unfortunately, even if you inadvertently stick with negative people, it will still wreak its havoc.

For this reason, if you discover that someone is gaslighting you, your best option would be to discontinue your relationship with them. You may be in a position where cutting off all ties may not be immediately practicable, but you should work toward that end.

Don't let past good experiences blind you from the unpleasant experiences an abusive person is presently putting you through. You need to move past sentimentalism and be more decisive to regain your freedom and rebuild your life again.

If you have suffered emotional abuse, especially gaslighting, you may conclude that you are frail, pathetic, and won't be able to take on the challenge of doing without the gaslighter in your life. Don't believe that lie. It is the gaslighter's spiteful narrative that is trying to trick you into losing faith in yourself. You are not frail or pathetic. Instead, you are strong because it takes a solid individual to survive gaslighting abuse. Don't let anyone tell you otherwise!

And no, you are not paranoid or too sensitive if you think that your colleague or business partner is undermining you. You are also not mistrusting if you feel that your spouse or romantic partner is being unfaithful. If you have a hunch, follow it without making accu-sations.

The gaslighter may have tricked your conscious mind, but they can't squelch your unconscious mind. This is why even though you may buy into their lies, you still feel an inner discordance with your truth. Trust your gut. Many mysteries have been unfolded, and cases have been solved based on nothing but a hunch. You may not be right all the time, but the more you listen to your intuition, the stronger it gets, and the more you trust yourself.

Ridding yourself of a gaslighter creates a vacuum in your life that needs to be filled. I am not suggesting that you should jump from an abusive relationship into the next available relationship. However, as you eliminate the bad influence from your life, it is wise to replace it with something empowering. Never neglect the need to stay in constant touch with a support system that will help to boost your sense of self. Get connected to support groups, trusted friends, and dependable family members from who you can draw inspiration. Leaving an abusive person without finding a favorable substitute does little to speed up your recovery and makes you vulnerable. Your journey to recovery is only assured with the help of positive reinforcements.

Remember that the bulk of your work is internal and intangible but carries a lot of impacts. Ending your relationship or friendship is necessary in most cases, but it is physical and external. Blocking an abuser's phone number, deleting their contact details, and severing all forms of communication is necessary, but there are all physical and external. You can still undo these things. But recognizing your true self-worth, building your self-esteem, learning to love and trust yourself more are intangible, internal, and have more influence on your behavior.

You can physically end a relationship but still want to be with the person despite causing you so much pain. But if you learn to recognize your worth, you would not desire to be with someone who treats you with disdain. So, become committed to the practices and exercises suggested in this book. They are your bedrock for recovery.

It is time to bid farewell to the confusion, self-doubt, and people-pleasing behavior forced down on you by the gaslighter. No one deserves to go through such insidious psychological torture—not you, not anyone!

I congratulate you for coming this far. You have begun a journey that may take several twists and turns, but don't be discouraged and worried about what lies ahead. If it feels overwhelming, perhaps you are trying to move faster than you should. Start with baby steps and when you think more surefooted, take the next logical step.

Here's to your success and speedy recovery!

Printed in Great Britain
by Amazon